CLASSIC
COUNSELS

CLASSIC COUNSELS

Soul-Stirring Topics from the Finest
Messages of the Prince of Preachers

C. H. SPURGEON

THE WAKEMAN TRUST * LONDON

CLASSIC COUNSELS

© Wakeman Trust 2003

THE WAKEMAN TRUST
(UK Registered Charity)

Website: www.wakemantrust.org

UK Registered Office
38 Walcot Square
London SE11 4TZ

US Office
300 Artino Drive
Oberlin, OH 44074-1263

ISBN 1 870855 42 6

Cover design by Andrew Sides

Printed by Stephens & George, Merthyr Tydfil, UK

These chapters consist of
sermons and shorter addresses of
C. H. Spurgeon, abridged and edited over recent
years for the *Sword & Trowel* magazine
(founded by Spurgeon in 1865).

Editor: Dr Peter Masters

Contents

1
Certain Assurance for Believers
Pearls of evidence for faith

'These things have I written unto you that believe on the name of the Son of God;
that ye may know that ye have eternal life, and that ye
may believe on the name of the Son of God'
(1 John 5.13).

IT IS FAR better to know that we have eternal life than to be able
to predict the future of empires or to forecast the destiny of
kings. John acts according to his loving heart when he writes to
lead us into the sure knowledge of our salvation. To whom was this
epistle written? It is important to note this, for I may be reading a
communication meant for somebody else. John wrote to *all those
who believe on the name of the Son of God.*

At one point John says, 'I write unto you, little children.' Then he
says, 'I write unto you, young men.' He also says, 'I have written
unto you, fathers.' Overall, he writes to babes, young men, and
fathers under the one comprehensive description of those who have
believed in the name of the Son of God.

Little children, you who have just begun the spiritual life, we want
you to be certain that you have eternal life. Young men, battling

with sin, we want you to be strengthened for your conflict by knowing that you have eternal life. Fathers, let us hope you have not come so far along the pilgrim journey without this knowledge, but these things are written so that you, in your mature years, may be certain that the life of God is strong within you. No person, young or old, is excluded from this text, unless he is an unbeliever. We may gather from the fact that John speaks exclusively to the people of God, that there are some true believers who are not certain that they have eternal life. A very large number of true believers do not know this cheering fact. For instance, certain Christians believe that even if they are now saved they may yet be lost. But John says firmly, 'Beloved, I pray for you that you may know that you *have* eternal life, and not a temporary life.'

The life which the Holy Spirit imparts to the believer is not a thing of days and weeks. It is eternal. We were born again to a living hope on the day of our regeneration. We were – 'born again, not of corruptible seed, but of incorruptible'. Our Lord at the well of Samaria gave us another figure: 'Whosoever drinketh of the water that I shall give him shall never thirst; but the water that I shall give him shall be in him a well of water springing up into everlasting life.' Many imagine that this spring can fail!

How much comfort God's dear children lose by not understanding the absolute immortality of the new life! Has not Jesus said, 'I give unto them *[my sheep]* eternal life; and they shall never perish, neither shall any man pluck them out of my hand'?

Still, there are Christians who believe all this, and are perfectly right in theory, but yet they cry, 'I want to know that I have eternal life. I want a fuller assurance of salvation than I have already obtained.' That is also our desire for you. John states as a fact, that everyone who believes on the name of the Son of God has eternal life. We should not doubt this. It is not a matter of inference and deduction, but a matter of revelation from God. You are not to form an opinion upon it, but to believe it, for the Lord has said it.

Listen to *1 John 5.1*: 'Whosoever believeth that Jesus is the Christ is born of God.' Thus says the Spirit of God, and so it must be. We do not need any further evidence. This is the unvarying testimony of the whole of Scripture. Many times John insists that the believer has eternal life. I beseech you never to question the statement. Settle it in your mind, for if you have any doubt about it you have undermined the Gospel. Glorify God by believing His testimony.

It is a very remarkable thing that people should not know whether they believe in Jesus or not: for it is easily ascertained. I know what I think. I know what I resolve. I know whether I doubt. I ought, therefore, to know whether I believe. But human nature received a terrible twist at the Fall. There is no estimating the possible inconsistency and contradiction of the human mind.

I have been in a state of mind in which I have questioned the possibility of there being a grain of grace in me, and yet I have clung to Jesus with a death grip. At such times my mind has worked morbidly, and its way has been turned upside down. Bunyan speaks of being 'much tumbled up and down in his thoughts'. It is possible for a person to be a very strong believer and yet to question whether he has a spark of faith. If you once become a sufferer under this wretched complaint, the absurdity of your disease will not lessen its painfulness. Our mental distresses need not be logical to be full of anguish. You probably know some people who are excessively nervous. They are afraid the skies will fall, or the earth will crack. This is certainly foolish, but the agony they suffer is very real.

It is necessary for me to say that full assurance of our possessing eternal life is possible. The Church of Rome teaches that no man can be assured that he has eternal life, except some few to whom supernatural revelations may be given. This sort of doctrine also lingers in the air of Protestantism. People who *know* that they have eternal life do not need to spend time in weighing and calculating evidences and perpetually examining themselves. I go a little further: it is our *duty* to obtain full assurance. We are commanded to give diligence to make our calling and election sure. I am convinced that it is right for a child of God to know that God is his Father, and never to have a question in his heart as to his sonship. I am certain it is right for a soul that is married to Christ to know the love of the bridegroom, and never to tolerate a cloud of suspicion to come between the soul and the full enjoyment of that love.

How does John help us in his epistle to know that we are believers, and consequently to know that we have eternal life? I cannot attempt a full résumé of it, but I shall select a few items. Without the slightest forcing of a single sentence it could be shown that the whole letter bears upon assurance. The exhortation of the apostle – that all believers might know that they have eternal life – is the silken thread upon which its pearls are strung.

First, believers ought to know that they have eternal life, and ought never to doubt it, because God's own word assures them that it is so. Remember that word of the Lord Jesus in *John 6.47* – 'Verily, verily, I say unto you, He that believeth on me hath everlasting life.' Will we doubt the Lord's 'Verily, verily'? Christ's word (unsupported by any external evidence) is quite enough to satisfy every gracious mind. 'Let God be true, but every man a liar.' Everything that we have looked upon as evidence of our standing should be regarded as a lie if it denies the declaration of the Lord.

Out of this simple faith in God, assurance comes naturally, by the operation of the Spirit of God upon the heart. Take pure, unadulterated milk and let it stand, and you will soon get cream. When faith has stood long enough, you see the rich cream of holy confidence upon the top of it. The witness of God is true, and therefore to be believed, and believed with full assurance. Do friends assure me that they see spiritual life in me? I am much obliged to them, but I do not need their evidence. 'He that believeth . . . hath the witness in himself.' When the Holy Spirit has made a statement, it is an impertinence to offer any further evidence upon the point. Therefore, that matter is not my subject. I take it, we must not offer you any other argument to prove the eternal life of believers beyond this – God has said it.

The only evidence which matters is this – 'Do I truly believe in Jesus Christ?' Let us look at the epistle for help in this enquiry.

1 You will find, first, that John mentions as an evidence of believing, *truthful dealing with God in confession of sin.* Normally, people walk in falsehood towards God, but when we have believed in Jesus we come to walk in the light of truth. 'If we say that we have no sin, we deceive ourselves, and the truth is not in us. If we confess our sins, he is faithful and just to forgive us our sins, and to cleanse us from all unrighteousness.'

The person who walks in the light comes before God as a sinner, whom the blood of Jesus Christ His Son cleanses from all sin. So, then, you may take this as an evidence that you are a saved person, if you deal truthfully with God, and if you confess your guilt before Him, your only hope for cleansing being the blood of Jesus Christ. If this is so then you have come to act towards God in the light of truth, and He accepts you.

The third chapter speaks of *purification.* 'Every man that hath this hope in him purifieth himself, even as he is pure.' Do you every day endeavour to keep clear of sin; and, when you have sinned, do you at night go with bitter repentance to God, and beg to be delivered from it? Are you fighting against your besetting sins? Do you contend against the customs of the world? Let that be an evidence that there is in you a new spirit which was not there by nature, and let that prove to you that you are quickened into newness of life.

2 Next, John gives us *obedience* as a test of the believer. In the second chapter, he says, 'And hereby we do know that we know

him, if we keep his commandments. He that saith, I know him, and keepeth not his commandments, is a liar, and the truth is not in him. But whoso keepeth his word, in him verily is the love of God perfected: hereby know we that we are in him. He that saith he abideth in him ought himself also so to walk, even as he walked.'

Come then brethren, do you obey the will of the Lord from your heart? Is holiness the aim of your life? Do you strive to do as Jesus bids you? Do you set your clock by the heavenly sun? Do you try to order your ways and your steps according to the law of the Lord? Do you delight yourself also in the law of God after the inner man? Then His servant you are Whom you obey. Rest assured beyond all question that you are one of Christ's sheep, for He says, 'My sheep hear my voice, and I know them, and they follow me.' 'He that doeth righteousness is righteous.' If grace has made you obedient it has given you eternal life.

3 I call attention, next, to the evidence of *love in the heart*. In the second chapter we read, 'He that saith he is in the light, and hateth his brother, is in darkness even until now. He that loveth his brother abideth in the light, and there is none occasion of stumbling in him.' Then go on to the third chapter. 'We know that we have passed from death unto life, because we love the brethren. He that loveth not his brother abideth in death.' This will greatly help you to decide your case. Do you hate anybody? Are you seeking revenge? Are you unforgiving? Then you are not dwelling in the light: you are of Cain and not of Christ.

We must feel a general benevolence towards all men, and a still more intense love towards all who are in Christ. This love must be practical, and lead us to help and succour our brethren. Have you this love? Do you feel a delight in the company of the brethren because they belong to Christ, however poor or illiterate they may be? You would not feel love reigning in your spirit if true faith had not come to dwell there. A loving spirit evidenced by a loving life is a true sign that you belong to God, Whose name is love. Be of good courage and enter into full assurance, all you whose hearts glow with the sacred flame of fervent love to God and men.

4 Next comes *separation from the world.* In the second chapter we read: 'Love not the world, neither the things that are in the world. If any man love the world, the love of the Father is not in him.' This is backed up by a sentence in the third chapter: 'Therefore the world knoweth us not, because it knew him not.'

Have you met with opposition from the ungodly? Do you find when you go out to work that your colleagues who used to drink with you are inclined to avoid you? Then there is a difference between you and others, and the world can see it. The serpent's seed will hiss at the seed of the woman. God has put an enmity between the two. Did not our Lord say, 'If the world hate you, ye know that it hated me before it hated you. If ye were of the world, the world would love his own: but because ye are not of the world, but I have chosen you out of the world, therefore the world hateth you'? Thus slander, abuse, and other form of persecution may be turned to your comfort by showing that you are of that sect which is everywhere spoken against.

5 Next to that, in the second chapter, we have the evidence of *continuance in the faith.* 'And the world passeth away, and the lust thereof: but he that doeth the will of God abideth for ever. Little children, it is the last time: and as ye have heard that antichrist shall come, even now are there many antichrists; whereby we know that it is the last time. They went out from us, but they were not of us; for if they had been of us, they would no doubt have continued with us: but they went out, that they might be made manifest that they were not all of us.'

Perseverance in holiness is a sure mark of election. It is the righteous who hold on their way; but mere pretenders are as wandering stars and fading flowers. That which comes and goes is not of God: the Holy Spirit abides permanently in true believers.

6 Furthermore, we find an evidence for true belief in *answers to prayer*: 'And whatsoever we ask, we receive of him, because we keep his commandments, and do those things that are pleasing in his sight.' Does God hear your prayers? Then you are pleasing in His sight. Are you in the habit of speaking with Him, and does He reply to you? Then you are agreed with God. He hears not those who wilfully live in sin; but if any man does His will, him He hears. You may look upon every answered prayer as another token of the love of God toward you in Christ Jesus your Lord.

7 *Adherence to the truth* is another help to assurance. Read the whole fourth chapter: 'Beloved, believe not every spirit, but try the spirits whether they are of God: because many false prophets are gone out into the world.'

If you have taken Scripture to be your guide, and hold fast by the truth of God, you are one of Christ's sheep, of whom He says, 'A stranger will they not follow . . . for they know not the voice of strangers.' He that questions what the Spirit says has not the Spirit of Christ dwelling in him. Against the detestable spirit of this age, and against everything that would corrupt the Gospel of Christ, it is the mark of the true seed to stand opposed.

8 One of the best evidences of true faith, and one of the best helps to full assurance is a *holy familiarity with God*. Read in the fourth chapter – 'And we have known and believed the love that God hath to us. God is love; and he that dwelleth in love dwelleth in God, and God in him. Herein is our love made perfect, that we may have boldness in the day of judgment: because as he is, so are we in this world. There is no fear in love; but perfect love casteth out fear: because fear hath torment. He that feareth is not made perfect in

love. We love him, because he first loved us.'

Eternal life is surely in you if you have entered into the secret place of the tabernacles of the Most High, and abide under the shadow of the Almighty. When you have no longer that slavish fear which makes you stand back, but that childlike confidence which draws you nearer and yet nearer unto God, then are you His child. The spirit of adoption is one point of sure witness from the Spirit of God.

* * * * *

Finally I wish to say personally, it is some thirty-four years since I first believed in Christ Jesus. I came to Him as nothing in myself, and I took Him to be my all. At this moment I possess a comfortable and clear assurance that I have eternal life. But my ground of confidence today is exactly what it was when I first came to Christ. I have no confidence in my confidence. I place no reliance upon my own assurance. My assurance lives in the fact that 'Christ Jesus came into the world to save sinners,' and that 'Whosoever believeth in him hath everlasting life.' I do believe in Him, and therefore I know I have eternal life.

Brethren, do not stir beyond that. Keep to your first faith. If you think it wise to examine these signs and evidences which I have given you, do so. But if you think you will get food out of them you will find a bare cupboard. If you think you can live without Christ, and without the daily exercise of faith, you tragically err. If you think you can live on what you have known in the past, you are greatly mistaken. It is like trying to live on stale manna. Everything you look to apart from Christ will rot in due time, so that you will loathe it. Every vessel, whether it be a great flagon or a little cup, must hang upon the one nail where it is fastened. If you wander from Jesus Christ, you wander into a land of darkness and of the shadow of death.

According to all right principles, assurance should increase by the

lapse of time during which faith occupies itself upon the sure promise. I have trusted my soul on Christ, therefore I have eternal life.
How do I know? I know, because the Spirit of God has so declared it
in the Word of God. Thus He has spoken – 'He that believeth on the
Son hath everlasting life.' I believe on the Son, and, therefore, I have
eternal life. I am a sinner, and Jesus Christ came to save sinners, and
they that trust in Him are saved. Therefore I trust Him. Therefore I
am saved. The Word of God declares it. Blessed be His name for
ever and ever.

2

Assurance for Doubting Seekers
Waiting for signs and wonders

'This is an evil generation: they seek a sign'
(Luke 11.29).

READING THE Old Testament, we observe that the Lord in former times graciously gave signs to His servants when He saw that it would be for their good. Moses, when he was called to undertake the great work of bringing the chosen people up out of Egypt and conducting them into the promised land, was given a sign to assure him that he was truly called of God. He put his hand into his bosom, and when he took it out it was leprous, white as snow. He thrust it into his bosom again, and again removed it, and lo! it was whole as the other. He cast his rod upon the earth, and the rod became a serpent. When he took it by the tail, it stiffened into a rod again.

So also in the case of Gideon, when he was commanded to go against the Midianite oppressors of Israel. You remember how his fleece was wet, when all around was dry; and how the sign was then reversed. When all around was saturated with moisture, the fleece was dry. In the cases of holy men favoured with signs, great faith was already in their hearts, and a real desire for more faith. There was a readiness to obey God. But the work to which the men were called was peculiar, difficult, and even super-human, and in view of the weakness of the flesh, God in His infinite tenderness gave them signs and wonders that they might be strengthened thereby.

Doubtless if there should come again a necessity for signs to prepare any of God's servants, such tokens would be given them. If there should ever be a time when it was not possible for Christians to walk by faith alone, or when it would be more to the honour of God that their confidence should be assisted by marvels and tokens, then God would operate once again in an extraordinary way, and His people would receive miraculous seals. If it were utterly impossible for the anxious and truly penitent spirit to find rest without a sign, I believe the sign would be given.

However, I also believe that *in no case is such a thing necessary under the Gospel dispensation,* which is so enriched with the plainest evidence, that to add more would be to hold a candle to the sun, or to pour water into the ocean.

In addition to this first remark, let us add that numerous signs have been given which have not wrought faith in those who have seen them. Signs alone do not lead to belief. Israel in the wilderness saw great marvels wrought by the Lord their God, and yet perished in unbelief. Pharaoh is a still more notable instance. What signs and wonders God wrought in the fields of Zoan! The Nile was crimsoned into blood, and all Egypt was filled with lamentation. The Lord turned the dust of the land into lice, and the ashes into plagues.

He brought up frogs into their chambers, and locusts devoured their fields. He darkened the heavens at midday, and deluged them with hail and rain such as the land had never seen before. A grievous murrain fell upon their cattle, and death upon their first-born. Yet all the wonders which God wrought did not soften Pharaoh's heart. Though for a while he trembled, yet he steeled himself against the God of Israel and said, 'Who is the Lord, that I should obey his voice?'

My hearers, if you do not believe Moses and the prophets, and if you do not believe in Jesus Christ on the strength of the testimonies already before you, neither would you believe if one rose from the dead, or if all the plagues of Egypt should be repeated upon you with tenfold fury. There is no necessary connection between the seeing of wonders and believing in God, for we learn clearly from Pharaoh's case, and from many others, that all the displays of wonderful power, either of judgement or of mercy, do not produce faith in unbelieving hearts.

I come to deal with a class of person very common in all congregations where the Gospel is faithfully preached. First, I shall describe the persons who constitute an 'evil generation' that seek after a sign. We have among us many individuals who are aware that they are sinners to the extent that they are very uneasy about their condition. They perceive clearly that sin will be punished by the Great Judge, and they are afraid of the wrath to come. They anxiously desire to find salvation; and, having long listened to the Gospel, they know the way of salvation.

They are not unbelievers in any of the doctrines of the Gospel. They accept the deity of Christ, and believe Him to be the Son of God Who died upon the cross, and offered atonement for iniquity. They know that this atonement is effectual for the putting away of transgressions, and that if they had an interest in it, it would wash away their sins and give them peace of mind. You will say to me, 'Knowing all this, of course they are believers in Christ.' No, they are not. We are very hopeful of them. We are at the same time very alarmed about them. They are not believers, for they wilfully persist in demanding some sign or wonder within themselves, or around them, before they will personally put their trust in the Lord Jesus.

Having been taught all they have been taught, and accepting as truth all that they do accept, the logical inference would be that they are trusters in Christ, and are saved. But, illogical as their state is, they still remain unbelievers, and justify their unbelief by telling you that if they felt this, or if they saw that, or if this happened, or if the other thing occurred, then they would believe in Christ personally, but not until then. They make different demands. There are some, and these are generally the most uneducated, who expect to experience remarkable dreams, or to see unusual visions. I am sometimes astonished that the notion persists that a certain kind of dream, especially if it be repeated a number of times, and if it be so vivid as to remain upon the imagination for a long period, is an indication of divine favour.

Nothing can be more baseless and without the shadow of evidence. And yet many imagine that if they suffered so grievously from indigestion that their sleep was spoiled by vivid dreams, then they could put their trust in Jesus Christ. The notion is absurd, and yet I have known many who have been, and still are, slaves to this delusion.

Not very long ago, after preaching in a country village, I was earnestly sought as a spiritual adviser by a woman who ascribed to me much greater wisdom than I ever claimed to possess. When I went to her house I found her very sick. I was saddened to find her the victim of a superstition, in which, I fear, her minister had comforted and confirmed her. She solemnly informed me that she had seen something standing at night at the bottom of her bed. She was hopeful that it was our blessed Lord, but she could not see His head. As I knew so much of spiritual things, could I tell her who it was?

I said I thought she must have hung up her dress on a peg on the wall at the bottom of her bed, and in the dark had mistaken it for an apparition. Of course, that did not satisfy her. I fell at once in her estimation to the level of a very earthly-minded man, if not a scoffer, but I could not help it. I was obliged to tell her it was nonsense for her to hope for salvation because she fancied that she saw Jesus with her bodily eyes, because saving sight is a *spiritual* sight. As to the question of the supposed apparition having a head, I urged her to use her own head and heart in meditating upon the Word of God.

There may have been, I will not deny it, dreams, and even apparitions, which have aroused the conscience, and so led to the commencement of spiritual life. But that such things are to be looked for and to be expected, is as far from the truth as the east is from the west. What if you did see an apparition or dream, what would it prove? It would prove nothing except that your imagination was morbidly active. Put such things away, they are primitive superstitions not fit for Christians. There are always some who will not believe Christ's simple Gospel unless absurdities such as this can be brought into it. May God deliver us from such unbelief.

Others we have met with think that in order to be saved they must feel some very peculiar physical sensation. Of course, the joy and peace, and the sheer discovery of the Gospel when it first flashes on the mind, may produce extraordinary sensations in the body, through the force of mental elation. But, I urge you, always remember that the grace of our Lord Jesus Christ has nothing to do with nerve, muscle, and sinew. It has nothing to do with things which may be seen or felt in the flesh. The operations of grace are a mental, spiritual work.

You must never imagine that when we talk about the heart we mean that central organ within us, from which the blood circulates. The work of the Holy Spirit concerns itself with the mind, the affections, the spirit. His work is altogether spiritual. God forbid that you should look for any strange effect on the body, such as some speak of. You must not put physical contortions or sensations as a test before the Lord, and say you will not believe in Him without them.

I hope these cases of people wanting bodily sensations are rare, but I have frequently met with people who will not believe in Jesus Christ for salvation because they have not felt wretched enough. They have read in certain books of godly men who, when they were seeking a Saviour, were broken in pieces under the hammer of the law. They turn to such biographies, and they find the subjects of them uttering language similar to that in *Job*, or in *Lamentations*.

Now these were good and holy men, and the way by which they were led to Christ was a way trodden by many. But none should say, 'Unless I can feel just the same, unless I can be led into despair, unless I can be tempted to destroy myself, unless I feel so miserable that I am unbearable, I cannot believe in Jesus Christ.' Poor demented friend, to desire misery and wretchedness as a kind of preparation for faith in Jesus Christ is a most insane thing! And yet many persist in unbelief because they think they are not yet wretched enough to trust Him.

Running to the other extreme, I have met with those who would not trust Christ because they were not happy enough. They have heard of the Christian's joys, and the peace like a river that abides for ever, and they have said, 'If I could only get this peace; if only this deep calm ruled in my spirit, then I could believe.' They might as well say, 'If I could only see the wheat fully grown in the fields of my soul, then I would begin to sow.'

Peace of mind is the *result* of faith, but they demand the result before they exercise the faith. They virtually ask God for the wages before the work is begun, demanding peace before they will believe. Believe me, if any of you act in this way, you must not imagine that God will turn aside from His wise and fixed procedure just to gratify your whims.

I have met with some who would not believe in Christ because they could not pray eloquently. They have said, 'If I could pray like So-and-So, to whom we have listened with such pleasure at the prayer meeting, then I could put my trust in Christ, and there would be some hope for me!' Praying fluently is sometimes only the result of oratorical gifts. If you will not believe in Christ until you get such gifts, you will never believe. How foolish you are to shut yourself out from Heaven because you cannot play the orator. Because you cannot be a preacher, you refuse to be a saint! True, fluency in prayer may also be the result of great depth of piety, but you must not expect to have great piety before you have begun to feel grace in your soul.

Before you put your trust in Christ, and become a babe in His family, you want to be a man six feet tall! Before you learn the A-B-C of the language of Canaan, you insist that you should be able to pronounce the hardest words. 'O madness, to what height wilt thou not mount!'

I have known others who must feel precisely as certain eminent saints felt many years after their conversion, or else they cannot believe that they are saved. They will read the life of some holy man who had mastered his passions by long years of mortification, and who had come to live very near to God, and they will mentally vow, 'I must be just like this man, or else I cannot believe in Jesus.' They say, in fact, to the Heavenly Physician, 'I am sick and ready to die, but, Good Physician, You must make me as strong as Samson at once, or I will not take Your medicine.' Well, this is marvellous, and truly, if there is anything on earth as wonderful as the mercy of God, it is the perversity of man, and the impudent way in which unbelief sets up one demand after another as an excuse for rejecting the Lord Jesus Christ.

We have met this mischief at other times in yet another shape. Says the young seeker, 'You tell me that if I simply put my trust in Jesus I shall be saved; but is not salvation a great mystery?' Our reply must be, 'Without doubt, it is.' In the light of which the seeker decides to wait until he receives some feeling, or some mysterious phenomenon within himself, before he will feel assured of salvation. It is not to be denied that the saving work of the Holy Spirit in the soul is the highest of all mysteries, but it must never be forgotten that it is also one of the grandest of all simplicities. The mysteries of the Church of Rome are mock mysteries, rendered dark by the veil which she casts over Truth. Her incantations, paraphernalia and ceremonies obscure what is plain. This is a kind of mystery of which the Gospel knows nothing.

The mysteries of regeneration are not the product of human interference. They are 'natural' mysteries. Light, for example, is the greatest of all mysteries, yet considered practically, it is the commonest of all simplicities. When the sun's rising rays scatter the darkness, we are not mystified. Light is a great mystery, yet we need not go to college to learn to light a candle. We do not need to understand the theoretical basis of the telegraph to be able to use this instrument. It may be a mystery, but it is simple to operate.

So it is with the mystery of regeneration. It is so mysterious that no one can explain it, but it is so simple that everyone who believes in Christ has experienced it already. It is so mysterious that if the most learned tomes were composed to define it, all the writers in the world would fail in its definition. But it is so simple that whoever believes in Jesus Christ is born of God. The only mystery lies in the operation of the Holy Ghost Whose coming and going we cannot comprehend. If you believe, then you have felt the mystery. If you trust Christ, you possess the mystery. All that is meant in regeneration, and all that is contained in the work of the Holy Spirit, is already possessed by every soul that has believed in Jesus Christ and in Him exclusively.

But some would rather go to Abana and Pharpar, rivers of Damascus, than to the blood of Christ, to wash and be clean. They will say, 'I thought he would surely come and strike his hand over the place, and call upon the name of the Lord his God, and recover the leper.'

They cannot accept the simple word, 'Believe and live,' so grand is its simplicity. Most rejecters of the Gospel react from its simplicity. Signs and wonders are their desire. Their soul craves after things artificially mysterious. But the naked grandeur of the sublime mystery of faith they cannot perceive.

I shall now show the folly of such conduct. You are seeking a sign, such as these I have described. You seek that which is quite *unnecessary*. What do you want a sign for? You want, you say, a token of God's love. What token of God's love to you can possibly be needed now that He has given His only-begotten Son, first to live on earth, and then to die in extreme pain, the just for the unjust? I am embarrassed for you, that you should ask a token of God's love while Jesus Christ is before you, for here is such love as nothing can ever equal.

What do you want a sign for? Why, you say, to show that there is mercy for you. Why do you need a sign? The very fact that you are alive shows how merciful God is! Had He been unmerciful, He would have cut you down long ago, for what are you but a cumberer of the ground, with your heart full of vile ideas, at enmity against Him? I know you are like this, for if you were not, you would not be so hard to lead to faith. Yet you are spared by His mercy! Is not that proof enough? Furthermore, the Gospel is preached to you. You are told that 'he that believeth . . . shall be saved.' He must be a merciful God Who lets you hear such a Gospel, and Who bids me plead with you, as though Christ pleaded with you, that you would lay hold of Him.

Why, the Gospel itself is the greatest of signs and wonders. What can you possibly want more than that? Furthermore, some of you have relatives, sons and daughters, who have been saved. You are a witness to what grace has done for them. What more evidence can you require of the saving power and mercy of God? Evidently grace did wonders for them. What more do you want to convince you?

You are also asking for *useless* signs. You say you want to feel deep conviction of sin, or great joy from God. But how could this help you to believe in Christ? Your joy or sorrow might be no more than worldlings feel when their wealth increases or decreases. It might be a matter of mere excitement. It may even prove to be a delusion and your damnation. Christ is worthy of confidence, but your joys or sorrows are not worthy of confidence. They may be good or they may be bad. They may be hopeful or they may be delusive. Why desire these? In so doing you seek another foundation than that which God has laid. Your feelings are fickle things. *Believe* and live!

Are you not also seeking *unreasonable* things? To ask a sign from God when He pledges His word, seems to me to be out of all reason. You are a beggar, remember, and we have an old proverb that beggars must not be choosers. Above all, how dare a beggar demand a sign before he will receive a gift?

Suppose I am walking in the street and I am accosted by a hungry man. If I offer him a loaf of bread, is he to refuse to take it unless I will fly in the air, or help him to turn a stone into bread? 'Let him starve,' you will say, 'if he is so unreasonable as to demand a sign.' And yet that is just like you. You will not take the mercy which the Gospel freely offers you, which God even commands you to accept, unless some astonishing sign or wonder is wrought before you or in you. Let your folly appear more obvious still when I remind you that you are asking for *unpromised* signs. God has promised that everyone who believes in Jesus Christ shall live. He has promised to hear prayer. But He has never promised to give anyone a sign or a wonder. Yet you ask Him to give you a sign which He has *never* promised, and do not ask Him to give you eternal life, which He *has* promised. Foolishness indeed!

Some of you are seeking for *injurious* signs. That depression of spirit which some think would be such an encouragement to them, why, it is even sinful. Should I ask a sinful thing of God? To be distracted in my mind, and so depressed and melancholy as to make myself and all my household miserable – is this a good thing? Am I to ask God to give me such things in order to help me to believe?

Some have wanted even thoughts of suicide! Why, these are awful, and should not be allowed to persist in the mind. You ask a scorpion; you ask a stone; you ask a serpent, and you imagine that after having all these things, you will be more able to receive the bread of the divine blessing! God will deny you, I am sure, what you so foolishly want. Be content to be led to Christ in a gentler way. Be willing to be blown to Christ by the soft south wind. Do not ask for tempests. Be satisfied to be drawn by the cords of love, and by the bands of a Saviour. Demand not whips and chains. Enquire not for the thunders and lightnings of Sinai. Be satisfied with the call of Calvary.

Remember that some of you who cannot trust in Christ without miracles or dreams or feelings are seeking signs *which others have never had.* I will give you an instance or two from parable and real life. There stood the prodigal son feeding the swine, so hungry that he would fain have filled his belly with the husks. The thought crossed his mind, 'I will arise and go to my father.' What sign had he? He set off to seek his father's face. What sign had he, I ask? There does not appear to have been even an invitation sent, but he sought his father and he found forgiveness.

Take another case. Christ has likened seeking souls to the widow who sought help from the unjust judge. She cried to him, and continued to cry to him, until she gained her request. But what sign had she? If she had any sign, it was all negative; all from the opposite quarter. Yet on she went. Look at the Canaanite woman. She desired that her daughter might be healed. What sign had she? Christ said, 'It is not meet to take the children's bread, and to cast it to dogs.' Instead of a sign to help her it was a hard word to discourage her, but yet she won her desire. And why not you?

The poor woman who touched the hem of Christ's garment in the crowd, what sign had she of His willingness to help her? It was her own faith in Jesus that made her touch the hem out of which the virtue came. Wait not then for signs to be given to you when they have not been given to others, but do as others have done, and obtain the same blessing.

I shall now lay bare the sin of doubting, which really lies behind the desire for signs. In the first place, by this unbelief, *you make God a liar*. Is not this the testimony of the Holy Spirit, 'He that believeth not God hath made him a liar'? How do we treat liars? If they tell us a thing, we say, 'I doubt it,' and we ask for more evidence. The everlasting God declares that whosoever trusts His Son shall be saved, and you tell Him that you doubt it! You say, 'I cannot and do not believe it, and I need more evidence. I want a sign and a wonder.' You make God a liar!

Also, *you insult God's sovereignty*. He has a right to give signs or not, as He wills. But you say, 'You must give me a sign now, or else I will be lost. I will not have mercy if I cannot have it in my own way. Great God, I will not be saved unless I can feel as I want to feel. I have a whim in my mind as to how the work of grace shall be wrought, and if it does not begin as I think best, I will sooner make my bed in hell than accept Christ.' Fling away this pride of yours, and bow to God's sovereign sceptre, and say, 'Lord, save me as Thou wilt. I believe, help Thou my unbelief.'

I must also tell you that in demanding some sign you are acting the part of an *idolater*. What does an idolater do? He says, 'I cannot believe in an unseen God; I must have a golden calf or an image which I can see with my eyes and touch with my hands.' You say just the same. You cannot believe God's bare word; you demand something you can feel and see. But this is sheer idolatry. You rate your own dreams, feelings, emotions, or strange impressions, as more worthy of trust than even God Himself. You make them idols, and put them into God's place. So far as you can, you undeify the Deity.

Should you not tremble at such a crime as this?

Do you not see, even further, how you *crucify the Saviour*? Those who nailed His hands to the tree were not greater sinners than you are, who say to Him, 'Bleeding Saviour, I believe that Thou hast died on the cross; I believe that Thy blood could cleanse sin, but as for me, I cannot trust Thee to save me. I have no confidence in Thee. I cannot, will not trust Thee. I trust my husband, or my wife, but I cannot trust the Saviour. I trust certain other people, but I cannot trust my God, the Son of God exalted in the highest heavens.'

This amounts to crucifying Him. I know not what can be worse than this. The nails in His hands were not more cruel than this mistrust of His deep love and His divine power.

'You are unfair,' says a doubter. 'I do not mean that. I only want to see the work of the Holy Ghost in my soul.' Then I have another charge to bring against you. You want to trust in the work of the Holy Spirit instead of trusting in the work of Jesus Christ. There is no text in all the Bible which tells you to make the work of the Holy Spirit the foundation of your confidence. Nowhere is the Spirit's work, for all its glory, set forth as the ground for a sinner's reliance. If you try to put the work of the Spirit where the work of Christ should be, you grieve the Holy Spirit, for the very last thing that He would do would be to supplant the Lamb of God.

It is the Spirit's office and mission to glorify Christ. How, then, can He supplant Him? When you say, 'I cannot trust the blood, I cannot trust the righteousness of Christ, I must have something from the Holy Ghost to trust in,' you drive a wedge between the work of the Holy Spirit and the work of Christ, and this grieves the Spirit to the last degree.

I have thought over this subject carefully, and I have tried to present it earnestly, but I am conscious that when I have done my best, you will go on in this folly, and continue in this sin. I pray that it may not be so, and that the Holy Spirit will show you the danger you are in. Suppose you should die in the state you are in. You are almost saved. In some measure you are awakened. You have many good desires. Nevertheless, a person who is only *almost* saved will be altogether damned.

There was a householder who *almost* bolted his door at night, but the thief came in. A prisoner was condemned to be hanged, and was *almost* pardoned, but he hung on the gallows. A ship was *almost* saved from shipwreck, but she went to the bottom with all hands on board. A fire was *almost* extinguished, but it consumed a city. A person whose spiritual state is *almost* decided, remains to perish in the flames of hell.

So it is with you. Unless you believe, all the good desires and emotions you possess will be of no service to you at all, for 'he that believeth not shall be damned.' O seek the Saviour now, while the Gospel message comes with fresh power.

> *Soon that voice will cease its calling,*
> *Now it speaks, and speaks to thee;*
> *Sinner, heed the gracious message,*
> *To the blood for refuge flee;*
> *Take salvation,*
> *Take it now, and happy be.*

There is one other thing of which you are in danger. You may be spared death for years to come, yet your long delay in wholeheartedly believing may cause your conscience to become seared as with a hot iron. If you believe this very day, whatever you may have been, your sins will be forgiven in a moment, that is if you look to Christ on Calvary and trust your soul to Him. But if you insist on relying on good works, or preparations, or feelings, or signs, or anything other than Christ, it may be that the Holy Spirit will never strive with you again. Your conscience will become hardened, so that you, having been given up to these idols, will utterly perish. In these circumstances you will perish even though you are under the sound of the Gospel, with the light of the Gospel shining directly into your eyes. You will perish from the serpent's bite even as the brazen serpent is lifted high. You will perish of thirst even though the water of life runs rippling at your feet, because you are not content simply to stoop down and take it as God presents it to you. O that you would this very day end these follies and these sins, and believe in Jesus Christ, through the power of the Holy Ghost!

3

Clear Away the Obstacles!
Advising 'outsiders' and seekers

'Cast ye up, cast ye up, prepare the way, take up the stumblingblock
out of the way of my people'
(Isaiah 57.14).

HAPPY WERE those days when earth was a province of Heaven, when Heaven and earth were so closely linked together that no arduous roads were needed to reach the Father's bosom! Man was pure when God created him, and able to hold communion and fellowship with his Maker in the garden of delights. The earthly Eden was then the paradise of the Holy One.

Terrible was the day when sin entered the world and destroyed the union between earth and Heaven! There stood the paradise above with its gates barred. Between Heaven and the place where Adam fell there was a great gulf fixed, so that they who would pass from poor fallen manhood to God, could not cross the awful chasm. It seemed also that no one could come from the holy Heaven to bless sinful man with angelic visits. The communion which had once existed between man and God was totally suspended. It was not merely interrupted, for an interruption supposes the probability of its being restored or resumed, but the sin of man altogether destroyed his fellowship with God.

Glory for ever to the Man Christ Jesus, Who has undone what Adam caused. He sets the pearly gates wide open, never more to be shut, until the safety of the last elect soul shall be secured in everlasting glory. The causeway made between fallen manhood and the divine Creator has gates that are not merely left ajar for the anxious ones who desire to enter, but which are thrown wide open so that 'whosoever will' may pass through.

These gates were opened by the atonement of Christ. To open them, no strength of human merit is needed. God does not ask His people to *make* a road of communication between Himself and sinners, but He commands us to 'take up the stumblingblock', 'gather out the stones', remove the obstructions, and 'prepare the way' which He Himself has made.

The road to Heaven, although it is well paved and straight, has some rough places along it. There are stones and stumblingblocks to be taken out of the way. There are difficulties in the way, and we have the honour of being co-workers together with God, as instruments to the salvation of our fellow creatures. All that we are asked to do is to remove the stumblingblocks and hindrances which Satan has caused to lie in the heavenly road. It is our business to take these out of the way, and make a straight path for the feet of sinners that they may come to the Saviour.

The first stumblingblock is often heard. People say, 'If we come to hear preachers, we cannot understand what they say.' They tell us that ministers use elaborate phrases, and talk of things that are dark and mysterious. To clear this obstacle we will toil and strain our minds to obtain figure and metaphor so that the Truth shall come home and be clearly understood. We will endeavour, as much as lieth in us, to preach the Gospel plainly. This stumblingblock shall be taken out of the way, and people shall have the Truth in simple and undiluted form, so that they can understand it if they want to.

Here is another stumblingblock in the way of people. We bring them up to the door of the house of the Lord, and we invite them to enter. 'No,' they say, 'just look at the inconsistencies of Christians.' We must prepare the way and remove this obstacle.

Many people, in effect, say, 'We attended your church, but don't imagine that we shall ever become converts to your religion. Look at the conduct of such-and-such an elder; see the behaviour of many of your church members; note the careless indifference of such-and-such a deacon. Don't imagine that we shall agree with your teachings if these are the effects they produce.'

Hypocritical professors, mere formalists, those who nominally occupy a place in the church, but whose hearts are not in the holy cause, do great injury to the cause of Christ. Henceforth, let us seek to live the truly godly life. Let us walk purely and uprightly in the midst of an unbelieving and excuse-making generation. When we have taken this stumblingblock out of the way, people will probably point out another. Many of these are of their own invention, but what does it matter where the obstacle comes from? If it hinders salvation, let us remove it.

Objectors say next, 'You Christians are such a gloomy set! Scarcely one among you has a sparkle in his eye and a light step. Your beliefs lead you to live severe lives. I would not think for a moment of becoming a follower of your melancholy religion. You take away everything that I call joy and pleasure. I cannot come with you.' We will seek to remove this stumblingblock also. We will labour with all our might to remember and obey the apostolic precepts: 'Rejoice evermore.' 'Rejoice in the Lord alway: and again I say, Rejoice.' From now on unbelievers shall not know when we keep our fast-days, because when we fast, we will anoint our head, and wash our face and we will not appear unto men to fast. They shall no longer say that we are gloomy. We will have some of the most cheering words of any upon our lips. We will have a warm smile for all, wherever and whenever we meet them.

On a different tack, there are also obstacles in the way of earnest seekers. When God calls sinners to Himself, He often chastens them sorely by showing them the deep depravity of their hearts, the sinfulness of their sin, and the ruin in which they are involved. Then they become penitent seekers. Such people find, on trying to come to Christ, many stumblingblocks in their path, over which they often stumble.

If it is the duty of Christians to clear the way for the outer world, how much more is it their duty to clear the way for those who have been convicted of sin by the Spirit of God! A Christian should look upon the newly-broken heart with special concern and love. If 'there is joy in the presence of the angels of God over one sinner that repenteth,' ought we not also to rejoice when we see the stirrings of new life in a person? Then the exhortation of our text comes to us with great force: 'Cast ye up, cast ye up, prepare the way, take up the stumblingblock out of the way of my people.'

And what are the stumblingblocks in the path of awakened sinners? They are huge masses broken off the great rock of ignorance, lying across their path. Many a sinner is unable to come to Christ because of his ignorance of the nature of repentance. 'I cannot repent enough,' says he; 'I am afraid I do not repent aright. Oh, that I could repent as I ought to repent! If I could have as deep and heartfelt a repentance as I ought to have, then I think I could believe in Christ.' Then the person adds to this another error, 'Oh, if I could feel the same terror of the Lord that such a man as John Bunyan felt! Oh, if I could be shaken by the collar over the very mouth of hell, till my whole blood were curdled, then I think I could have hope!'

Then again, in the way of other seekers, the stumblingblock is the opposite. Such a one says, 'Oh, if my heart could have been opened gently, as was the heart of Lydia, then I could think there could be some hope for me.' Christian, when you hear such a tale as this (and I have heard many such), speak at once to that anxious soul, and tell him quickly that, 'This is a faithful saying, and worthy of all acceptation, that Christ Jesus came into the world to save sinners.' Tell him that God in Christ Jesus is the Saviour, that He brings some to Himself by thunders and lightnings, and some by a 'still small voice'.

If you see any in this kind of trouble, tell them that God is a God of variety. He saves one by one means, and one by another, so that the experiences of seekers are not all the same. Tell them that where one person is made to feel the Lord's judgements as a ton weight, another may feel them as the gentle droppings of the dew from Heaven. Say to them that there is a mighty tree which is said to open in flower with a report that makes the forest shake. Then remind them that the sweet flowers of the hedgerows open without any noise whatever. Bid them learn from the works of nature that there will be a sweet variety in the works of grace.

Cheer and comfort them by telling them that, if they come to Christ genuinely, they cannot come to Him the wrong way. They cannot come to Christ at all except the Father, Who has sent Christ, draws them, and the Father will never draw them the wrong way. Tell them that Jesus has said, 'Him that cometh to me I will in no wise cast out.' So, take up this obstacle out of the way of coming sinners, and tell them not to be distressed.

If they think they have not repented enough, tell them this is true, and that they never will repent enough. Tell them that *you* have not repented enough, and the brightest saint who has ever lived has not repented enough. Tell them it is not the *quantity* of their repentance, but its *quality* which is the proof of divine grace. Tell them, if they truly forsake their sins and believe in Christ, though their feelings may not be so acute as those of others, yet God will freely and fully pardon all who unfeignedly repent of their sins, and believe with the heart on His Son, Jesus Christ. Again I say to you, 'Take up the stumblingblock out of the way.'

Yet another person may come to you, and say, 'I am afraid I am not one of the elect. I know I feel my sin. I cry out to God for mercy. But this obstacle stops me – what if I should not be one of the elect? What if God should not have chosen me unto eternal life? Then my prayers must be in vain, and I must be for ever shut outside the gates of Heaven.' Let us take this stumblingblock out of the way. He that believeth on the Lord Jesus Christ *is* elect. Tell the fearing soul that whoever has faith in the Saviour, and is prepared to renounce all other confidences, and trust and believe in Christ crucified, is as surely elect as the glorified saints before the eternal throne.

Bid him make his 'calling' sure, for then shall his 'election' also be made sure unto him. Tell him, as a guilty sinner, to go to the Cross, and there prostrate himself, and look up to the wounds that bleed out new life for him. There, at Calvary, shall he learn the certainty of his election, and be no more troubled by his doubts upon that point.

You will find a thousand hindrances vexing the sinner when he is coming to Christ. Do your best, by kind words, by wise expositions of Scripture, by showing the real nature of the difficulties, to clear the way and take up every stumblingblock.

Let me press on one point further, and say that there are many stumblingblocks to be removed from the way of Christians. When people have exercised faith in Christ, and known that their sins are forgiven, the *whole* work of grace is still not accomplished. Certainly, the work of *salvation* is achieved, for, as Joseph Hart sings –

> *The sinner that truly believes,*
> *And trusts in the crucified God,*
> *A pardon at once then receives,*
> *Redemption in full through His blood.*

Still, it is not enough merely to be believers, to have our sins forgiven, and to be spiritually alive. Oh, no! The moment we are converted, we set out anew. We have gained the wicket gate, as John Bunyan has it, but the pilgrim's journey is not over. It has only just begun, and there is a long distance yet to be travelled. We are to make progress in our love to God, our search for knowledge and our advance towards holiness.

There are many stumblingblocks in the way of the Christian, especially the young Christian, and it is the duty of the Christian minister, and of all experienced Christians, to take up these stumblingblocks out of the way, that they may not hinder the progress of the children of God. Brethren and sisters, let us do all we can to smooth the path, and to clear the way for our fellow Christians. They will find the road rough enough, but let us do all we can to make it less rough. Our God, blessed be His name, 'stayeth his rough wind in the day of the east wind'. Although the road we travel must always be rough, He will not let the iron enter our soul to slay us, neither will He let the floods overflow and drown us.

> *A Christian man is seldom long at ease,*
> *When one trouble's gone, another doth him seize.*

I remember once seeing an old farmer stop his pony, and get out of his chaise to pick the bottom of a broken glass bottle off the road. Said he, 'I remember that my old pony cut its foot with an old glass bottle, and I should not like anyone to lose a valuable horse, so I thought I would stop, and get out, and throw the dangerous thing out of the road.' Let us do as the old farmer did.

There are many church members who are now gratified by the position they hold in the church. Do not forget that it was not always so with you. There was a time when you used to go up to the house of prayer, and no one spoke to you. You remember that deacon who held up his head very high, or else looked down upon you very condescendingly. There was a sister who passed by you with a patronising air, and never uttered a word. These were real stumblingblocks in your way. Your heart was often cut to the quick because no one spoke to you. There are many people today in the same position you were once in. Be very careful to notice them. Take up the stumblingblock out of *their way*. If you do not, you may unintentionally make their lives very unhappy.

You may at some time or other have felt the bitterness of being in need, and no one helped you. Go out now where believers are in great need and endeavour to relieve them. Take the stumblingblock out of their path, and do all that you can to lessen their troubles.

Do you know a Christian who is in error on some doctrinal subject? Take up the stumblingblock out of his way if you can, and show him the way of the Lord more perfectly, as Aquila and Priscilla did for Apollos.

You may know some brother or sister with a very tender conscience. Say nothing that can grieve them. There are some people in this world who seem to belong to a race quite peculiar to themselves, who appear to be here for no other reason than to cause themselves and others annoyance. You sit by their side, and they at once introduce a subject which creates discord. They always have something to which they object. They fancy there ought to be reform in all the churches. I dare say they think they would make good reformers; but I am afraid their kind of reformation would really mean destruction.

They probably like their own minister, but they would be pleased to set him right upon some points. They object to all their neighbours. One they cannot bear because he is too lax; another too firm in his principles, and a bigot. Such people as these are always casting stumblingblocks in the paths of others.

One of these hyper-critical friends had a son – let us call him William. He went one Sunday, and heard the minister, and a deep impression was made on the lad's mind. As he walked home, he said to his father, 'What a good sermon we had this morning!' 'Ah!

William,' answered the father, 'you think so, but that is your lack of experience; the doctrine was not sound.'

'I think, Father, the preacher was very earnest.' 'Oh!' replied the foolish man, 'there is a great deal of affectation in him. I don't think much of him, he is not the kind of minister I like, and not equal to the old preacher I used to hear in my young days.' The lad puts his hands in his pockets, and forgets all he has heard, and says to himself, 'Well, if this is what Father thinks of the sermon, I shall think no more about it. There is evidently not much in it to trouble my head about.'

What a huge stumblingblock this wretched business of criticising sermons and finding fault with ministers casts in the path of many an anxious soul! Brethren, take this stumblingblock out of the way of our hearers. The falls of Christians are grievous stumblingblocks. One falling Christian does more mischief than a hundred standing ones. There may be a hundred rivers flowing noiselessly on, and no one hears *them*. But there is one waterfall, the noise of which exceeds the sound of all the flowing streams.

Surely, it is the Christian's duty to be circumspect in his walk, that he may not cast this stumblingblock across his brother's path. If there is anything we are doing that might lead others to sin, let us be swift to abandon it. Let us not place any temptation in the way of others. Let us not make ourselves responsible for the consequences of sin in others by leading them into it through our example. 'Abstain from all appearance of evil,' is the inspired command of Scripture.

I conclude by portraying a Christian who is dying. He has lived in this world to serve his Saviour, and to serve his fellow Christians. He has often cherished the fatherless, comforted the widow, and strengthened the feeble. Now he comes to die. The pearly gates of the City of God are wide open to receive him. Who are those who approach him there with faces full of gladness? Let these white-robed spirits tell their own tale. They say, 'We are happy to welcome you into the mansions of the blessed, and to receive you into the everlasting habitations.' The saint replies, 'I know you not, bright ones; why do you so welcome me?' One answers, 'You do not know me now, but on earth I was a poor widow, and you came to my house when I was bereaved, and you poured the oil of consolation into my lonely heart.'

Another celestial spirit says, 'On earth I was a young man; do you not remember me? You gave me the opportunity to study. You encouraged and helped me in my labours, and I am glad now to meet you here.' Another says, 'On earth I was an old, grey-headed man who, with tottering steps, came into the place of worship, and you met me at the doors, and gave me a cordial shake of the hand, and said, "Come in, I am glad to see you." You took me into your seat, gave me a hymnbook and a Bible, and made me glad. You invited me into your home, you led me, as it were, into green pastures, and by the side of still waters, and you gave to my soul consolation, and now I am happy to welcome you to Heaven.' Let us thus labour, dear brethren and sisters, to help others. Surely, if such assistance once helped us to secure our own salvation, it is blessed to be instrumental in guiding others towards the heavenly kingdom. Let us labour to help each other, in temporal matters and in spiritual affairs. In every sense let us endeavour to 'prepare the way', and to 'take up the stumblingblock out of the way' of the travellers through this wilderness. That their path may be unimpeded, let us together resolve that we will clear the road of all that would hinder pilgrims heavenward.

May the Lord give His blessing to His own people, and grand abundance of grace unto us all, until we meet in the paradise above with Jesus our Redeemer!

(A weeknight message delivered in 1856, not included in the Metropolitan Tabernacle Pulpit.)

4

The Valley of the Shadow of Death
Sure relief for every downcast believer

'Yea, though I walk through the valley of the shadow of death, I will fear no evil: for thou art with me; thy rod and thy staff they comfort me'
(Psalm 23.4).

I INTENDED that this choice promise should be kept in store until I came near the river of Jordan, and then, in my last hours, I would enjoy its sweetness and sing with joy –

> *Yea, though I walk through death's dark vale,*
> *Yet will I fear no ill:*
> *For Thou art with me, and Thy rod*
> *And staff me comfort still.*

The other day I found that I needed to eat this heavenly loaf at once, and I did so. I drew honey out of it some days ago when a tempest howled around me, and I hope that every believer who is burdened and cast down may find it as precious as I have found it. This verse is no doubt very applicable to the experience of a believer when he comes to die, but it is for the living too, and if your soul is cast down within you, and you are walking through the valley of death-like shade, I invite you to consider its truths. The words are not in the future tense, and are not therefore reserved exclusively for a distant moment.

David was not dying. He is lying down in green pastures, and following his Lord by still waters; and if a cloud has descended upon him, and he feels himself as one threatened with death, he nevertheless expects goodness and mercy to follow him through all his days.

I call your attention, first, to the pass and its terrors – 'the valley of the shadow of death'. Get the idea of a narrow ravine upon the higher Alps where the rocks seem piled to heaven, and the sunlight is seen above as through a narrow rift. Troubles are sometimes heaped on one another, pile on pile, and the road is a dreary single-file pass or defile through which the pilgrim on his journey to Heaven has to wend his way. Set before your mind's eye a valley shut in with stupendous rocks that seem to meet overhead, dark as midnight itself. Through this valley or rocky ravine the heavenly footman has to follow the path appointed for him in the eternal purpose of the Infinite Mind.

Our first observation about it is that this ravine is *exceedingly gloomy* – its chief characteristic. It is the valley of the shadow of death. The joy of life has been like the sun under an eclipse; and in the chill, dark, damp shade of a terrible sorrow a believer has cowered down and shivered beneath the icy touch of doubt.

I speak to some young hearts who, I hope, know nothing about this gloom. Do not want to know it. Keep bright while you can. Be as larks, and mount aloft. But there are some of God's people who are not much in the lark line; they are more like owls. They sit alone and keep silence; or if they do open their mouths it is to give forth a discontented hoot. Such mournful ones need all the gentle sympathy we can afford them. But those who are cheerful do, many of them, occasionally pass through the dreary glen where everything is doleful; and their spirits sink. I know that wise brethren say, 'You should not give way to feelings of depression.' Quite right, yet we do.

'But surely,' you say, 'desponding people are very much to be blamed.' I know they are, but they are also to be viewed with compassion, and if those who blame them furiously could once know what depression is, they would realise the cruelty of scattering reproof where comfort is needed. There are experiences which are full of spiritual darkness; and I am almost persuaded that those of God's servants who have been most highly favoured have suffered more times of darkness than others.

The covenant was never known to Abraham so well as when a horror of great darkness came over him, and then he saw the shining lamp moving between the pieces of the sacrifice. A greater than Abraham was early led of the Spirit into the wilderness, and again before He closed His life He was sorrowful and very heavy in the garden. Blessed be God for mountains of joy, and valleys of peace, and gardens of delight; but there is a Vale of Death-shade, and many of us have traversed its tremendous glooms.

Our second observation is that this valley experience is *dangerous*, as well as gloomy. In journeying through the passes of the East an escort is usually needed, for robbers lurk among the rocks. The name of the Khyber Pass is still terrible in our memories, and there are Khybers in most people's lives. You that are beginners, I do not wish to frighten you; but on the way to Heaven there are 'Cut-throat Lanes' where, when the enemy finds your spirits down, he pounces with temptation, and before you know it you may be wounded. There are spots in the valley where every bush conceals an adversary, and temptations spring out of the ground like fiery serpents, and where the soul is among lions. If you have not yet come to that part of your pilgrimage I am glad of it, and I hope that you may be spared it in answer to the prayer – 'Lead us not into temptation.'

But if you are called to walk through this dangerous ravine what will you do? Say this to yourself – 'Yea, though I walk through that dangerous pass of which I have heard, I will fear no evil, for Thou art with me; Thy rod and Thy staff they comfort me.' You who are placed in positions of great trial and temptation need not wish for an easier pathway, for it may be that you are safer now, being on your guard, than those who are not fiercely tried, and are in peril from sloth and spiritual indifference. The cold mountains of trial can be safer than the sultry plains of pleasure.

Our third observation is that this terrible pass is *shrouded in mystery*. It is this that gives rise to the gloom. You do not always know what the depression is about. You cannot discern the form which broods over you. You cannot grasp the foe. It is of no use drawing a sword against a shadow. Bunyan represents the pilgrim as putting up his sword when he came into the valley of the shadow of death. He had fought Apollyon with it, but when he came into the midnight of that horrible defile it was of no use to him, because everything was so veiled and blackened in the dark. Hobgoblins, as he called them, hovered around – strange shapes and singular forms of doubts which he could not combat with reasoning or overcome with argument.

In the valley of shadow the believer does not know what the trial is, and yet a strange, joy-killing feeling is upon him. All is suspense, surmise, and uncertainty. That which frightened Belshazzar when the handwriting was upon the wall was the sight of the hand, but he could not see the arm and the body to which the hand belonged. So, sometimes we cannot understand God's dealings with us. We have come to a place where two seas meet, and we cannot discern the current. Such things happen to God's people now and then. And what are they to do when they get into these perplexities, these mysterious troubles, that they cannot at all describe? They must do as David did, who in the peace and confidence of faith went on his way singing to this effect – 'Yea, though I walk through the valley shaded by the mysterious wings of death, and though I know nothing of my way, and cannot understand it, yet will I fear no evil, for Thou art with me. Thou knowest the way that I take. There are no mysteries with my God. Thou hast the thread of this labyrinth, and Thou wilt surely lead me through. Why should I fear? Thy rod and Thy staff they comfort me.' Gloom, danger, mystery, these three all vanish when faith lights up her heavenly lamp trimmed with the golden oil of promise.

Our fourth observation is that the narrow pass is a *lonely, solitary* place. It is as if the traveller walked alone. Loneliness is a very great trial to some spirits; and some of us know a great deal of what it means, for we dwell alone. But you will say, 'Do you not mingle with crowds?' Yes indeed, and there is no loneliness like it. When your work sets you on a mountain all alone, you will know what I mean. For the sheep there are many companions; but for the shepherd few. Those who watch for souls often come into positions in which they are divided from all human help. No one can guess the burden of your soul.

Some of you are in a position in which you complain, 'No one was ever tried as I am.' Or possibly you murmur, 'There may be many who are more troubled than I am, but none in my particular way.' Just so – and that is an essential part of the bitterness of your cup, that you should lament that you are alone. But will you not say, with your divine Master, 'You shall leave me alone, and yet I am not alone, because the Father is with me'? Now is the time for faith.

When you trust God, *and a friend,* there is a question whether it is God you trust or the friend; but when the friend has left you, and only God is near, no question remains. If you and I are walking together, and a dog follows us, who knows which is the dog's master? But when you go off to the left and I turn to the right, all will see who owns the dog, by seeing whom he follows.

If you can trust God when you are utterly lonely, then you really trust Him; you are a believer and there is no mistake about it. It is profitable to be driven into loneliness, that we may prove whether we are solely trusting God or not. It is a bad thing to be standing with one foot on the sea and the other on the land. We must get both feet on the Rock of Ages, or the foot which stands upon the sea of changeful self will be our downfall. My soul, wait thou only upon God! Yea, though I walk through the dark valley, unattended by human companion, I will fear no evil, for my God is near.

Our fifth observation is that this dark valley is an *often-walked* pass. Many more go by this road than some people dream. Among those who wear a cheerful countenance in public there are many who are well acquainted with this dreary glen; they have passed through it often, and may be in it now. When I wear the sackcloth of sorrow, I try to wear it under my outer garments where no one shall see it, for has not the Master said, 'Thou, when thou fastest, anoint thine head, and wash thy face; that thou appear not unto men to fast'? Why should we cast others down? There is enough sorrow in the world without our spreading the infection by publishing our troubles.

Story books are sent me to review, and when I perceive that they contain harrowing tales of poverty, I make short work of them. I see quite enough of sorrow in real life; I do not need fiction to fret my heart. If men and women must write works of fiction at all, they might as well write cheerfully, and not break people's hearts over mere fabrications. Some like to tell the story of their sorrows. But if my own heart is bleeding why should I wound others? Sometimes it is brave to be speechless, even as the singer puts it –

> *Bear and forbear, and silent be;*
> *Tell no man thy misery.*

It is surely true that a great number of God's best servants have trodden the deeps of the valley of the shadow; and this ought to comfort some of you. The footsteps of the holy are in the valley of weeping. As surely as this Word of God is true, your Lord has felt the chill of the death-shade. He says, 'Reproach hath broken my heart; and I am full of heaviness.' The footprint of the Lord of life is set in the rock for ever, even in the valley of the shadow of death!

Our sixth observation is that this valley, dark and gloomy as it is, is *not an unhallowed pathway*. No sin is necessarily connected with sorrow of heart, for Jesus Christ our Lord once said, 'My soul is exceeding sorrowful, even unto death.' There was no sin in Him, and consequently none in His deep depression.

We have never known a joy or a sorrow altogether untainted with evil; but grief itself is not necessarily sin. A man may be as happy as all the birds in the air, and there may be no sin in his happiness; and a man may be exceeding heavy, and yet there may be no sin in the heaviness. I do not say that there is not sin in all our feelings, but still the feelings in themselves need not be sinful. I would, therefore, try to cheer any brother who is sad, for his sadness is not necessarily blameworthy. If his downcast spirit arises from unbelief, let him cry to God to be delivered from it; but if the soul is sighing, 'Though he slay me, yet will I trust in him,' it is not a fault.

If the man cries, 'My God, my soul is cast down within me: therefore will I remember thee,' his soul's being cast down within him is no sin. Heaviness of spirit is not, therefore, on every occasion a matter for which we need condemn ourselves. The way of sorrow is not the way of sin, but a hallowed road sanctified by the prayers of myriads of pilgrims now with God – pilgrims who, passing through the valley of Baca, made it a well.

The second part of this discourse will consider the attitude of the pilgrim as he passes through his valley. First, we notice that *the pilgrim is calm about what lies ahead*. The outriders of trouble are often of a fiercer countenance than the trouble itself. We suffer more in the dread of trial than in the endurance of the stroke. Here we have a man of faith who is calm in the expectation of trouble: 'I shall walk,' says he, 'through the valley of the shadow of death. I expect to do so, but I will fear no evil.'

Have you, my friend, a trouble drawing near to you? Then look bravely at the future. Let not your heart fail you while waiting for the thunder and the hurricane. David said, 'Though an host should encamp against me, my heart shall not fear: though war should rise against me, in this will I be confident.'

Encamped enemies generally trouble us more than actually contending foes. When once the enemy raises the war-cry, and comes on, we are aroused to valour, and meet him foot to foot, but while he tarries and holds us in suspense our heart is apt to eat into itself with perplexity. Pray to be calm in the prospect of trial: it is half the battle. Is it not written of the believer, 'He shall not be afraid of evil tidings: his heart is fixed, trusting in the Lord'?

Secondly, we see that *the pilgrim is steady in his progress.* 'Yea, though *I walk* through the valley,' says he. He does not run in haste: he walks quietly along. We are generally in a hurry to get our trouble over. Cries one, 'I feel in such a horrible state of suspense that I must end it one way or another.' But, my dear friend, faith is not in such a frightful bustle, for – 'He that believeth shall not make haste.'

Faith is quick when it has to serve God, but it is patient when it has to wait for Him. There is no flurry about the psalmist. 'Yea, though I walk,' says he – quietly, calmly, steadily. So David in effect declares – I shall walk through the valley of the shadow of death as quietly as I walk my garden in the evening, or go down the street about my business. My affliction does not ruin me for duty, I am not flurried and worried about it. May God give you, my dear brothers and sisters, this calm faith. I pray that He may give it to me, for I greatly need it.

Thirdly, we see that *the pilgrim has a certain expectation.* He says – 'Yea, though I walk *through the valley.*' There is a bright side to that word 'through'. He expects to come out of the dreary pass to a brighter country. He says within himself, 'I shall come out on the other side. It may be very dark, and I may go through the very bowels of the earth, but I am bound to come out on the other side.' So is it with every child of God.

If his way to Heaven should lie over the bottom of the sea, hard by the roots of the mountains where the earth with her bars is about him, he will traverse the road in perfect safety. Providence makes special preparation for every tried saint. If you are God's servant, and are called to trial, some singular providence the like of which you have never read of shall certainly happen to you to illustrate in your case the divine goodness and faithfulness. Oh, if we had more faith! Let us be sure that if we walk in at one end of the hollow way of affliction we shall walk out at the other. Who shall hinder us when God is with us?

Fourthly – and this is the main point about this pilgrim and his passage through the valley – we see him *renouncing all fear*. He says, 'I will *fear* no evil.' It is beautiful to see a child at perfect peace amid dangers which alarm all those who are with him. I have read of a little boy who was on board a vessel buffeted by the storm, and everyone was afraid, knowing that the ship was in grave danger. There was not a sailor on board, certainly not a passenger, who was not alarmed. This boy, however, was perfectly happy, and was rather amused than frightened by the tossing of the ship. They asked him why he was so happy at such a time. 'Well,' he said, 'my father is the captain. He knows how to manage.'

He did not think it possible that the ship could go down while his father was in command. There was folly in such confidence, but there will be none in yours if you believe with an equally unqualified faith in your Father, Who can and will bring safely into port every vessel that is committed to His charge. Rest in God and be quiet from fear of evil.

Fifthly, we note that this pilgrim, in divesting himself of fear, is *not at all fanatical or ignorant,* since he gives good reason for his attitude. 'I will fear no evil,' says he, 'for thou art with me.' Was there ever a better reason given under Heaven for being fearless than this – that God is with us? He is on our side. He is pledged to help us. He has never failed us. Where, then, is there room for terror when the omniscient, immutable God is on our side? Let the heavens be dissolved, and the earth be melted with fervent heat, but let not the Christian's heart be moved: let him stand like the great mountains, whose foundations are confirmed for ever, for the Lord God will not forsake His people or break His covenant.

'I will fear no evil: for thou art with me.' There is something more here than freedom from fear and a substantial reason for it, for the true believer *rejoices in exalted companionship.* 'Thou art with me.' Thou – Thou – Thou – the King of kings, before Whom every seraph veils his face. 'Thou art with me.' How brave that person ought to be who walks with the Lion of the tribe of Judah as his guard!

Trembling brother, you would feel perfectly safe if you had your eyes opened to see the companies of angels that surround you. You would rejoice in your security if you saw horses of fire and chariots of fire encompassing you. But such defences are as nothing compared with those which are always around you. God is better than myriads of chariots. 'The chariots of God are twenty thousand, even thousands of angels'; but the glory of it is that 'the Lord is among them, as in Sinai.'

God is with every one of His children. We dwell in Him, and He dwells in us. 'I in them, and they in me,' says Christ. A vital, everlasting union exists between every believing soul and God, and what cause can there be for fear? 'Thou art with me.' Oh for grace to be courageous pilgrims, and to make steady progress with heavenly company as our glory and defence.

5
Young Believers and Spiritual Food
How converts are sustained in life

'Then shall the lambs feed after their manner'
(Isaiah 5.17).

THE OLD HEBREW commentators considered 'the lambs' to mean the house of Israel, and regarded this as a promise that in all times of distress and affliction God's flock would still be fed. Whether that be the correct sense or not, I shall use the words as having some such meaning. Our text deals with the lambs, and to the lambs we intend to speak. Young converts, new-born souls – these words are for you: *you* shall feed after your manner.

Our first observation is, *that young believers must feed.* Simple enough observation certainly, and clearly to be inferred from the common course of nature, for no sooner is any living thing created than there are procedures for its feeding. No sooner is a seed cast into the ground and vitalised than it gathers to itself the particles upon which it feeds. No sooner is an animal born than it receives food. Surely the Lord does not create life in the regenerated soul without providing stores upon which it may be nourished. Where

He gives life He gives food. I have been very anxious, beloved, that you should be diligent in the service of God, and I have continually stirred you up, not to be sitting listening to sermons when you ought to be doing good. The consequence has been that some have gone forth to do good whom I should not have exhorted to do so, because for them it would have been better if they had waited a while till they had learned more, both of doctrine and experience. Young brethren, there is a time for feeding as well as a time for working. We do not allocate to little children the work of heavy labouring. Some lesser service in the house is suitable for them, and will do them good; but we do not exact too much from them, for we know that youth is a time in which they must be learning and growing.

Therefore let me say to some of you who know little or nothing of your Bibles, or of your own hearts: Wait a little, and do not run before you are sent. Sit still a while at Jesus' feet, and learn what He has to say to you, *then* run as a messenger with a real message. It could be that at this moment you have more foot than heart and more tongue than brain, and this is sad.

Let us not forget that our souls need to be fed. Look at many Christian people – what do they do? What is their reading? The daily paper! I condemn it not, but of what use is this to their souls? What do they read to nourish the inner life? And beyond reading, what else do they do to nourish their spirits? Our fathers would go into their chamber three times a day and take a quarter of an hour for meditation. How many today maintain such a habit? Is it done once a day?

It was my privilege to live in a house where at eight in the evening every person, from the servant to the master, would have been found for half-an-hour in prayer and meditation in his or her chamber. As regularly as the time came round, that was done, just as we took our meals at appointed hours.

In the old Puritan times a servant would as often answer, 'Sir, my master is at prayers,' as he would nowadays answer, 'My master is engaged.' It was then looked upon as a recognised fact that Christian men did meditate, study the Word, and pray, and society respected the interval. It is said that in the days of Cromwell if you had walked down Cheapside in the morning you would have seen the blinds down at every house at a certain hour.

When will God's people perceive that it is not enough to be born again, but that the life then received must be nourished daily with the bread of Heaven? It is not enough to be spiritually alive. All Christians should know that they must sit down to their heavenly Father's table until He has satisfied their mouths with good things and renewed their strength like the eagle's.

The more intensely earnest we are in feeding upon the Word of God, the better. My young friends, you require to be fed with knowledge and understanding and therefore you should search the Scriptures daily to know the doctrines of the Gospel, and the glories of Christ. You will be on the right track if you read the *Confession of Faith* and study the proof texts; or learn the *Shorter Catechism,* comparing it with the Book of God from which it is derived. Especially in these days, when people are so readily drawn into false teaching, we need to know what we believe.

Protestantism grew in this land when there was much simple, plain, orthodox teaching of the doctrines which are assuredly believed among us. Catechising was the very bulwark of Protestantism. My young friends, may you obtain a spiritual understanding of God's Word which is more than knowledge. May you discern the inward sense, compare spiritual things with spiritual, and see the relation between this truth and the other.

May you also be fed by mingling with the saints of God and learning from their experience. Many a young Christian gathers from advanced saints what he would never discover elsewhere. As they tell of what they have felt and known and suffered and enjoyed, the lambs of the flock are strengthened and consoled. Seek the company of those who can instruct you. It is a barren thing for a young man to associate only with those who are below him in experience, and not with those from whose lips pearls drop, because they have been in those deeps where pearls are found. Be much with experienced Christians and you will be fed by them.

Young friend, *much feeding will come to you by meditation upon the truth that you hear.* As the cattle lie down and chew the cud, so does meditation turn over the truth and get the very essence and nutriment out of it. To hear and hear and hear as some do is utterly useless, because, when they have heard, it is all over as far as they are concerned. It has gone in one ear and out of the other, and has left nothing upon the mind. Turn the things you hear over in your mind to explore them.

Secondly, the text says that the lambs shall feed 'after their manner'; and that leads us to observe that *young believers have their own way of feeding.* There are several lessons that may be drawn from the way lambs feed. They feed on tender grass. Young Christians love the simple truths of the Gospel. No father excludes a child from his table when he is three or four years old because he is not yet able to speak Latin. If the little ones know their A B C, it is a good beginning.

We think a great deal of the first little verse our babes repeat. They say it in such a strange way that nobody thinks it is language at all except father and mother, but they are charmed with the simplest form of speech which infant lips can try. So to see a little spiritual knowledge in new converts should gratify us, and cause us to love them. Leave the lambs to feed on tender grass, and you older ones may take as much of the tougher herbage as you like.

Thirdly, *lambs like to feed little and often.* They are not able to take in much at a time, but they like to be often at it. I love to see our young people coming to the prayer meetings and weekday services so continually. You will grow in grace if you are often engaged in the means of grace. But it is possible to make such things a weariness to the flesh if they become protracted. Strong saints can bear whole days of devotion, and delight in them, but for young believers, let them have here a little and there a little, a text and a text, line upon line, precept upon precept – but let them have it often. 'Then shall the lambs feed after their manner.'

Fourthly, *the lambs, if they feed well, feed after their manner, quietly.* If there is a dog in the field they will not feed. If they are driven about hither and thither, and not allowed to rest, they cannot feed. I pity young Christians who get into churches where there are disturbances and troubles. Oh, may we ever be kept at peace! I bless God for the love that has reigned among us. May it continue, and may it deepen! Beloved friends, when we fall out with one another we shall find that the Spirit of God has fallen out with us. We cannot expect to see young converts among us at all, much less can we hope to see them advance in grace, if we indulge a party spirit, or a controversial spirit within the fold.

All believers should endeavour to maintain a sacred quiet within the church for the sake of the younger ones. You will have heard of the child who was greatly impressed by a sermon, and resolved to pray on reaching home. But he heard his father and mother on the road home discussing the sermon, and finding such fault with it that the happy season of tenderness passed away from him. In later years he often said that his becoming an unbeliever was due to that conversation. Let the lambs feed quietly.

There are certain people who seem to be cut on the cross, and the only use they are in this world seems to be to raise irritating questions. They, and the mosquitoes, I suppose were created by infinite wisdom, but I have never been able to discover the particular blessing which either of them confer upon us. Those who discuss and discuss, and nothing else, had better be let alone.

Fifthly, *when lambs feed after their manner, they feed in pleasure.* A very disorderly lot the lambs are, if you look over the gate at them. They are never proper and solemn. An artist can scarcely sketch them for their friskings and gambols. Young Christians ought not to be told to cease their sanctified humour. They ought not to be expected to groan with those that groan just yet, but allowed to rejoice with those that do rejoice. Their days of sorrow will come soon enough. For now let them rejoice in the Lord.

Excited enthusiasm in the church is by no means to be deprecated in young converts. I remember Dr Fletcher say that he once saw a boy standing on his head, dancing on the pavement, and displaying all sorts of antics of joy. He said to him, 'Well, my lad, you seem to be exceedingly merry.' He replied – 'I am, and so would you be, Guv'nor, if you had been locked up three months, and had just got out.' I thought this very reasonable indeed.

When an unbeliever has felt the grief of sin, and has been shut up in the prison of the law, and Jesus Christ comes and brings him out, and he begins to rejoice with joy unspeakable and full of glory, should his exuberance and enthusiasm be curbed? 'Let the lambs feed after their manner.'

Sixthly, *when the lambs feed after their manner, they feed in company.* They like to get with others if they can. Sheep thrive best in flocks. I call upon every young Christian here to get into some part of Christ's flock. I invite you into this portion of Christ's church, but if you find any other where, all things considered, you think it would be better for you to be, go there.

Mind that you join yourself first to Christ, and after that with His people. Do not try to go to Heaven as a solitary individual. By companies Christian people proceed towards the New Jerusalem. May you have much love to the visible church, and believe that, notwithstanding all her faults, there is none like her in the earth.

Seventhly, I must close with the remark that *in the worst of times God will see that His lambs and the rest of His flock are fed*. It is said, 'Then shall the lambs feed after their manner,' that is, when the vineyard was destroyed and the hedge broken down; when thorns and briars had come up, and the clouds had refused to rain, and God had sent desolation upon Israel, and the people were gone into captivity – even then shall the lambs feed after their manner.

This is a blessed truth, that, come what may, God's people shall be saved, and they shall have spiritual meat. There may come persecuting times. Never mind. Never did Christ seem so glorious as when He walked with His church in the dungeon and up to the stake. Never were there sweeter songs than those which rose up from the Lollards' tower and Bonner's coal-hole. Never did the church have such marriage feasts as when her members died at the gallows and the fire. Christ Jesus has made Himself pre-eminently near and dear to a persecuted church.

Therefore fear not, if you should have your portion of trouble to bear in your family; or hostility and shame from an evil world, for you *shall* feed after your manner. Though your parents should be annoyed by your stand; though your husband should be angry; though your brother should ridicule; though your employer should scoff, you shall be fed with spiritual meat, and your soul shall surmount all these ills, triumphant in her God.

'But I fear,' says one, 'that there will come times of sickness to me. I have premonitions of it.' Yes, but you shall be fed after your manner. And I for one bear witness that sometimes periods of sickness are times of the greatest spiritual nourishment. The Lord can furnish a table in the wilderness. Sickness is certainly a 'wilderness' by itself, but God will give you daily manna. He can make you strongest in heart when you are weakest in body. Therefore fear not, God will *feed* you.

'I am afraid of poverty,' says one. Are you? That has been the lot of many of God's people. For centuries now the Lord has chosen the poor to be His disciples. You need not fear that. Your Master too experienced it. You will never be so poor as He was, for He had not where to lay His head. Fear not, He will feed you.

'Ah, but I fear death,' says one. Even in the valley of the shadow of death you will find tender grass. Have you never seen others die? Has it not been a remarkable thing to see some saints depart? I bring to your minds those who have recently ascended, whom we loved. Was there anything terrible about their deaths? Did they not smile upon us in their last hours?

I have often seen young persons getting ill with consumption, and heard from them strange things that made me think them half prophets or seers whose eyes have been anointed so that they looked within the veil, and saw the glory of the invisible. Oh, how texts of Scripture have been placed in golden settings by dying saints! How sweetly have they set promises to music!

Do not talk about monks and their illuminated missals! Scripture illuminated by dying saints is far more marvellous. What amazing joy believers have felt! Some have even said that the joy was killing them, not their disease. It was as though the great floods of glory had burst their banks, and the soul was being swept right away to eternal bliss. It has been such a blessing to die that it is foolish – perhaps wicked – for any Christian to be afraid to depart. 'Then shall the lambs feed after their manner' – feeding near the very scythe of death, and cropping choice morsels at the grave's mouth.

We shall soon disperse, as this congregation has done hundreds of times, and go each one to his home. Shall we ever meet again? Possibly we shall never again see some in the body. But never forget that we are a flock, and we must gather again in one meeting place before the judgement-seat on that day of wrath, that dreadful day. Shall we meet then as the sheep of Christ, or be divided, to the right and to the left, as the sheep of the great King, or the goats condemned to be cast away? We shall meet there certainly, but will it be an eternal meeting of unending joy? God grant it may! But there can be no union at the throne, except there first be union at the cross. Will you come to the cross? Will you trust the Redeemer? Will you bow before Him? Will you be washed in His blood? Will you be saved with His salvation? If so, we shall all meet in Heaven to see the face of the Lamb in His glory. And there shall the lambs feed safely and supremely and eternally after their manner.

(A short discourse from *The Sword and the Trowel,*
November 1876, not included in the
Metropolitan Tabernacle Pulpit.)

6

The Pinnacle of Faith
The example in the offering up of Isaac

'And he said, Take now thy son, thine only son Isaac, whom thou lovest, and get thee into the land of Moriah; and offer him there for a burnt offering upon one of the mountains which I will tell thee of'
(Genesis 22.2).

I DO NOT intend to enter into this narrative in its bearing upon our Lord, although we have here one of the most famous types of the Only-begotten, Whom the Father offered up for the sins of His people. We shall dwell now upon the triumph of Abraham's faith when his spiritual life had come to the highest point of maturity. After he had passed through nine great trials, each of them most searching and remarkable, and had through the process been strengthened and sanctified, he was called to endure a still sterner test.

It is good to learn that God does not put heavy burdens on inexperienced shoulders. He educates our faith, testing it by trials which increase little by little in proportion to our faith. He only expects us to endure adult afflictions when we have passed through the childhood state and arrived at mature stature in Christ Jesus. Do not think that as you grow in grace the path will become smoother beneath your feet, and the heavens serener above your heads. On the contrary, reckon that as God gives you greater skill as a soldier, He will send you upon more arduous enterprises. As He more fully fits your vessel to brave the tempest and the storm, so will He send you out upon more boisterous seas and longer voyages, that you may honour Him more.

You would have thought that Abraham in his old age, after the birth of Isaac, would have had a time of perfect rest. Let this warn us that we are never to reckon upon rest from tribulation this side of the grave. No, the trumpet still sounds the note of war. We shall now look at *the trial itself;* we shall next see *Abraham's behaviour under it;* and shall, in conclusion, spend a little time in noting *the reward which came to him* as the result of his endurance.

1 The Trial

There is scarcely a single syllable of God's address to Abraham in the opening of this trial which does not seem intended to pierce the patriarch to the quick. 'Take now *thy son,* thine only son.' What! a father slay his son? Was there nothing in Abraham's tent that God would have apart from his son? The patriarch would cheerfully have given Him all his herds. All the silver and gold he possessed would have been readily surrendered. Will nothing satisfy the Lord but Abraham's son? If one must be offered of human kind, why not Eliezer of Damascus, the steward of his house? Must it be his son? How this heaves at the father's heart-strings!

The word *only* is particularly emphasised by the fact that Ishmael had been exiled at the command of God. If Isaac shall die, there is no other descendant left, and no probability of anyone else to succeed him; the light of Abraham will be quenched, and his name forgotten. Nor is that all: 'Thine only son *Isaac*.' What a multitude of memories that name 'Isaac' awoke in Abraham's mind. This was the child of a promise graciously given, the fulfilment of which had been long and anxiously expected. Isaac, the child of the covenant, the child in whom the father's hopes all centred, was the gift of God who was to be retracted. Surely this was a trial of trials!

There was more heartache still, for the Lord added the words, *'whom thou lovest'*. Must Abraham be reminded of his love to his heir at the very time he is to lose him? The phrase seems to have no bowels of compassion in it. Was it not enough to take away Isaac, without at the same moment awakening the affections which were so crushed?

Isaac was very rightly beloved of his father, for in addition to the ties of nature, and his being the gift of God's grace, his character was most lovely. His behaviour at the time of his sacrifice proves that in his spirit there was an abundance of humility, obedience, and resignation, and such a character was quite sure to have won the admiration of his father.

But note, not only was this tender father to lose the best of sons, but this son must be sacrificed *by the father himself*. If the Lord had said, 'Speak thou with Eliezer, and charge him to offer up thy son,' it would have softened the trial, but Abraham must grasp the sacrificial knife and drive it into the breast of his son, and then see him consumed to ashes upon the altar. Everything was designed to make the trial severe. The friend of God was tried in such a way as probably never fell to anyone before or since.

In addition to the sacrifice, Abraham was commanded to go to a mountain which God would show him. It would have been agony to obey at once while under the fresh influence of sacred impulse, but to have three days to chew this bitter pill would have been a triple agony. He must journey on with that dear son before his eyes each day. Only faith, mighty faith, could have assisted Abraham to look in the face the grim trial which now assailed him. He might have said, 'I am called upon to perform an act which violates every instinct of my nature. I am to offer up my child! Horrible! Murderous! I am to burn my slaughtered child as a religious act – terrible, barbarous, detestable! I am myself to offer him upon the altar deliberately. How can I do it? How can God ask me to do that which tears up by the roots every one of the affections which He Himself has implanted, which runs counter to the whole of my humanity?'

We too may be called by the Word of God to acts of obedience which seem to us to violate all our natural affections. Christians are sometimes commanded to come out from the world by decided acts, which provoke the hatred of those who are nearest and dearest. Now, if they love God, they will not prefer father nor mother, nor husband, nor brother, nor sister, in comparison with Him; and though Christians will ever be among the most tender-hearted of people, they will be ready to give up all for His sake. They will deny every natural affection sooner than violate the divine law.

Perhaps, today you are suffering under an affliction which is grieving all the powers of your nature. The Lord has been pleased to take away from you one dearer than life, for whom you could have been well content to die. O, learn with Abraham – let not Isaac stand higher than the Lord. Let Isaac be dear, but let Isaac go sooner than God be distrusted. Bow your head and say, 'Take what Thou wilt, my God; slay me, or take all I have, but I will still bless Thy holy name.' This was how Abraham's love for God was demonstrated.

It may have occurred to Abraham that he would, by the slaughter of his son, be rendering all the promises of God futile. There are times with us also when we are called to a course of action which looks as though it will jeopardise our highest hopes. A Christian is sometimes bound by duty to perform an action which, to all appearance, will destroy his future usefulness.

I have often heard men advance as an argument for staying in a corrupt church, that they have obtained an influence there, which they would lose if they followed their conscience and left. True Christians, however, must be ready to forfeit all their supposed influence, and renounce their apparent advantages, rather than sin against their conscience, just as Abraham was bound to offer up Isaac, in whom all the promises of God were centred.

It is neither your business nor mine to fulfil God's promise, nor to do wrong to produce the greatest good. To do evil that good may come is false morality, and wicked policy. Our duty is to obey God, and He will take responsibility for the fulfilment of His promises, and the preservation of our usefulness. Though He dash my reputation into shivers, and cast my usefulness to the four winds, yet if duty calls me, I must not hesitate a single second. At the command of God, then, Isaac must be offered because obedience can never endanger blessings, and God's commands are never in real conflict with His promises, because God can raise up Isaac and fulfil His own decree.

Abraham *must* have been subject to the thought that the death of Isaac was the destruction of all his comfort. The tent would be darkened for Sarah, and the plain of Mamre barren as a wilderness for her lamenting heart. He must have felt thus, but it did not make him hesitate. Sometimes the course of duty may lead through the death of our dearest comfort and our brightest hope. But we must do right, come what may.

It must also have occurred to Abraham that from that time forth he would make himself many enemies. Many would distrust his character, count him a wretched person, and shun him as a murderer of his own son. How could he bear to meet Sarah again? 'Where is my son?' How could he meet his servants again? How could he bear their looks, saying, 'You have slain your son'? How could he face Abimelech and the Philistines? The wandering tribes which roamed about his tent would all hear of the awful murder and shudder at the thought of the monster who defiled the earth on which he trod. And yet observe the holy detachment of the godly man to what might be thought or said of him. Let them count him a devil. Let a universal hiss consign him to the lowest hell of hatred and contempt, he takes no account of it, for God's will must be done. God will take care of His servant's character. He must obey, for no second course is open to him, and he will not consider disobedience.

This is one of the grandest points about the faith of the father of the faithful; and if you and I shall be called to exhibit it, may we never be found wanting. May we be ready to brave calumny and reproach with cheerfulness, through the power of the Holy Ghost. How Luther's lips must at first have trembled when he ventured to say that the Pope was Antichrist. The millions bowed down before the 'vicar of God on earth'. 'No,' said Luther, 'he is Antichrist, and a very devil.'

When he found himself shunned by the ecclesiastics who once had courted his company, and heard the common howl that went up, that the monk was a drunkard, and (when he married a nun) was filled with lust, he said, 'They may call me what they will, but I know that God has spoken into my soul the great truth of salvation by faith in Jesus Christ. I will not hold my tongue.'

2 Observing the patriarch under trial

In Abraham's bearing during this test everything is delightful. His obedience is a picture of all virtues in one, blended in marvellous harmony. First notice the *submission* of Abraham under this temptation. There is no record of any answer given by Abraham. It had been a startling command, 'Take thine only son, and offer him for a burnt offering!' But Abraham does not argue the point. It is natural to expect that he should have said, 'But, Lord, do You really intend it? Can a human sacrifice ever be acceptable to Thee? Thou art love and kindness. It cannot be.' But there is not a word of argument; nor a solitary question that even looks like hesitation. 'God is God,' he seems to say, 'and it is not for me to ask Him why, or seek a reason for His bidding. He has said it: I will do it.'

Prayer against so dreadful a trial might not have been sinful. He could have prayed, 'My Lord, for Sarah's sake, and for Thy promise's sake, test me not so.' But from this grand soul there is no such prayer. He does not ask to escape; he does not pray to be delivered once he knows God's will. Much less is there the semblance of murmuring.

Abraham goes about this business as if he had been only ordered to sacrifice a lamb ordinarily taken from the flock. There is a coolness of deliberation about it which does not make him a Stoic, but does prove that he was gigantic in his faith. 'He staggered not,' says Paul, and that is just the word. You and I, if we had done right, might have done it in a staggering, hesitating manner; but not he. He knows that God commands him, and with awful sternness, and yet with childlike simplicity, he sets about the sacrifice.

The lesson I gather from this is: when you know a duty, never pray to be excused, but go and do it in God's name in the power of faith. If ever you clearly see your Master's will, do not wait for better opportunities: do it at once. It is a very terrible thing to delay or disobey, and to let conscience grow hard. It is like the freezing of a pond. The first film of ice is scarcely perceptible. Keep the waters stirring, and you will prevent the ice from hardening, but once let it film over, and it will thicken over the surface, until it is so solid that a waggon might be drawn over it. So with conscience, it films over gradually, and at last it becomes hard, unfeeling, and it can bear a weight of iniquity.

This world has come to a sad pass because of the tricks men play with their consciences. This is the cause of all those unnatural senses that people give to texts and creeds. This is the secret reason why the religion of this land, which claims to be Protestant, is becoming popish to its very core, because evangelical men have sworn allegiance to a popish catechism, and given it another sense. Instead of coming out of a corrupt church, they have dallied with their consciences, and by their practice have nullified their preaching and taught men to lie.

But we must move on to notice next Abraham's *prudence.* Prudence may be a great virtue, but often becomes one of the meanest of vices. Prudence rightly considered is a notable handmaid to faith; and the prudence of Abraham was seen in this, that he did not consult Sarah as to what he was about to do.

Naturally, prudence would have said that it was Sarah's due to give her judgement in the case, and that Eliezer, who had often helped and guided Abraham, should be consulted. 'Yes,' Abraham probably thought, 'but these beloved ones may weaken me.' And, therefore, like Paul, he did not consult with flesh and blood. After all, what is the good of consulting when we know the Lord's mind?

If I go to the Bible and see very plainly there that something is my duty, for me to consult with others as to whether I shall obey God or not is treason against the Majesty of Heaven. Imagine an inferior officer in an army, when ordered in the hour of battle to lead an attack, turning round to a fellow soldier to ask his opinion of the orders he has received from the commander-in-chief! Let the man be tried by court martial, he is utterly disloyal.

Notice, further, Abraham's *alacrity.* He rose up early in the morning. O, but most of us would have taken a long sleep, or if we could not have slept, we would have lain till dinner time at least, tossing restlessly. The command does not specify the hour; there is no peremptory word as to the time of starting upon the awful journey. At least let us postpone it as long as we may, for the dear young man's sake; let him live as long as possible.

But no, delay was not in the patriarch's mind. The holy man rises early. He will let his God see that he can be trusted, and that he will do His bidding without reluctance. O believers, always be prompt in doing what God commands you. Hesitate not. The very pith of your obedience will lie in your making haste and delaying not to keep the Lord's commandment.

Further, I must ask you to notice Abraham's *forethought*. He did not desire to break down in his deeds. Having cleft the wood, he took with him the fire, and everything else necessary to consummate the work. Some people take no forethought about serving God, and then if a little hitch occurs, they cry out that it is a providential circumstance, and use it as an excuse to escape the unpleasant task.

O, how easy it is when you do not want to involve yourselves in trouble, to think that you see some reason for not doing so! Says one, 'We must live. Why should I throw myself out of a job merely because of a small point of conscience?' Says another, 'I know the Bible says I ought to act differently, but we must take circumstances into consideration, and compel the postponing of obedience.' Abraham takes care as far as possible to forestall all difficulties that might prevent his doing right. 'No,' he says, 'there is no compromise for me, my duty is clear. Does God command it? I will provide all that is needful for the fulfilment of His will. I want no excuse for drawing back.'

Observe, further, Abraham's *perseverance*. He continues three days in his journey, journeying towards the place where he was to sacrifice his son. He bids his servants remain where they were, fearful perhaps lest they might be moved by pity to prevent the sacrifice. Now, you and I would have liked to provide ourselves with some friend who might have stepped in to prevent the deed, and to take the responsibility off our shoulders. But, no, the good man puts everything aside that may prevent him going all the way.

Then he puts the wood on Isaac. O, what a load he placed on his own heart as he lay that burden on his dear son! He bore the fire himself in the censer at his side, but what a fire consumed his heart! How sharp was the trial when the son said artlessly, 'My father, behold the fire and the wood: but where is the lamb?' He made but a short reply.

We have every reason to believe that other replies followed, which are not recorded, in which Abraham explained how the case stood, for it is hard to suppose that Isaac would have blindly yielded unless first an explanation had been given that such a command had come from the highest authority, and must be obeyed.

At last, Abraham unsheathes the knife, and the deed is about to be done, but God is content. Abraham has truly sacrificed his son *in his heart* and the command is fulfilled. Notice the obedience of this friend of God. It was not a matter of talking about what he would do, but his faith was practical and heroic. I call upon all believers to note this. We must not only love God so as to hope that we should be ready to give up all for Him, but we must be literally and actually ready to do it. We must ask for more faith, so that when the trial comes, we shall not be revealed as mere windbag pretenders, but true to God in deed.

How many professors love God until it comes to losing their pence and their pounds, and involves penury and poverty. Many will be faithful to God until it comes to scoffing and shame, and then they are offended, and thereby prove who is really their God. So many serve their God up to a certain point, but no further, and so show that they love not God at all.

I have but feebly brought into the light the obedience of Abraham, but I must not leave the scene until I have mentioned what lay at the bottom of it all. The eleventh chapter of *Hebrews* tells us that *by faith* Abraham offered up Isaac. What was the faith that enabled Abraham to do this? I believe that Abraham was sure in his own mind that God *could not lie*, and God's Word could not fail, and therefore hoped to see Isaac raised from the dead. He said to himself, 'I have had an express promise that in Isaac shall be my seed, and if I be called to put him to death, that promise must still be kept. God will raise him from the dead.' We are told in the New Testament that he believed in God that He could raise him from the dead, from which he also received him 'in a figure'.

Some may say, 'But this lessened the trial.' Granted, but it did not lessen the faith, and it is the faith which is most to be admired. He was sustained under the trial by the conviction that it was possible for God to raise his son from the dead, and so to fulfil His promise. But beneath this, there was in Abraham's heart the conviction that by some means, if not by that means, God would justify him in doing what he had to do; for it could never be wrong to do what God commanded him.

Brethren, believe that all things work together for your good, and that if you are commanded by conscience and God's Word to do that which would impoverish you or throw you into disrepute, it cannot be a real hurt to you, and it must be right. I have seen men cast out of work owing to their keeping the Lord's Day, or they have been for a time out of a job because they would not fall into the tricks of trade.

O for the faith which never will, under any persuasion or compulsion, fly from the field. If only people had strength enough to say, 'If I die and rot I will not sin, or do what God commands me not to do, or fail to do what God commands me to perform!' This is the faith of Abraham. Would God we had it! We should have a glorious race of Christians if such were the case.

3 The resulting blessing

Let us, then, observe *the blessing which came to Abraham* through the trial of his faith. First, *the trial was withdrawn,* for Isaac was unharmed. The speediest way to get to the end of tribulation is to be resigned to it. God will not try us when we can fully bear the trial. Give up all, and we shall keep all. Give up your Isaac, and Isaac shall not need to be given up. But if you will save your life, you shall lose it.

Secondly, Abraham had the *express approval of God*: 'Now I know that thou fearest God.' The man whose conscience bears witness with the Holy Ghost enjoys great peace, and that peace comes to him because under that trial he has proved himself a true and faithful servant. O brethren and sisters, if we cannot stand the trials of this life, what shall we do in the day of judgement? If we are afraid of a little loss and a little scorn, what would we have done in the martyr days, when men counted not their lives dear to them, that they might win Christ?

Abraham next had *a clearer view of Christ than ever he had before* – no small reward. 'Abraham rejoiced to see my day,' said Christ: 'He saw it, and was glad.' In himself ready to sacrifice his son, he had a representation of Jehovah, Who spared not His own Son. In the ram slaughtered instead of Isaac, he had a representation of the great Substitute Who died that men might live.

More than that, to Abraham *God's name was more fully revealed that day.* He called Him Jehovah-Jireh, a step in advance of anything that he had known before. 'If any man will do his will, he shall know of the doctrine.' The more you can stand the test of trial, the better instructed shall you be in the things of God. There is light beyond, if you have grace to press through the difficulty.

To Abraham that day *the covenant was confirmed by oath.* The Lord swore by Himself. Brethren, you will never get the grace of God so confirmed to you as when you have proved your fidelity to God by obeying Him at all risks. Then you will find how true are the promises, and how faithful is God. The quickest road to full assurance is perfect obedience. While assurance will help you to obey, obedience will help you to be assured: 'If ye keep my command-ments, ye shall abide in my love; even as I have kept my Father's commandments, and abide in his love.'

Last of all, God pronounced over Abraham's head *a blessing*, the like of which had never been given to man before. First in trial, he is also first in blessing. First in faithfulness to his God, he becomes first in the sweet rewards which faithfulness is sure to obtain. Brethren and sisters, let us ask God to make us like Abraham, his true chil-dren, that we may gain such rewards as he obtained. May He help us to make a surrender in our hearts of all that we have of the dearest objects of our affections. May we by faith take all to the altar today in our willingness to give all up, if the Lord wills.

May we never pause to ask whether any act of obedience shall make us rich or poor, honourable or despised, or whether it will bring us peace or anguish, but may we go right onward, as though God had shot us from the eternal bow, in the firm conviction that if there be temporary darkness, it must end in everlasting light. Let us set our seal upon the fact that God is true, that rewards are to the righteous, and true peace to the obedient, and that in the end it will be our highest gain to serve God. O that there may be trained in this house a race of much enduring believers, who can endure hardness, but cannot endure sin.

May you, my brethren, obey your convictions as constantly as matter obeys the laws of gravitation, and never may you sell your birthright for the world's wretched pottage. Could this house be filled with such men and women, London would shake beneath the tramp of our army, and this whole land would perceive that a new power had arisen up in its midst. The Lord make us true men like Abraham, true because believing, and may He help us to sacrifice our all, if need be, for Jesus' sake. Amen.

7

Places of Entertainment
Discernment in the matter of amusements

*'Come out from among them . . . and touch not
the unclean thing; and I will receive you'
(2 Corinthians 6.17).*

W E HAVE GREAT reason to bless God for the rich mercies we have enjoyed as a church and people for many years, in the unity of the brotherhood, the zeal of the workers, the number of conversions, the success of all our enterprises, and the growth of the whole body. It is on my heart to say a word upon another subject – a subject which presses heavily upon my heart. I beseech you, by the mercies of God, and by the love of Christ Jesus your Lord, that as members of this church you do nothing which would grieve the Spirit of God, and cause Him to depart from among us.

Remember how Israel suffered defeat because of Achan. One man only, and one family only, had broken the divine rule, but that sufficed to trouble the whole camp. Achan had taken of the accursed thing and hidden it in his tent, and so all Israel had to suffer defeat.

Churches, too, will suffer if sin becomes general among them and is allowed to go unrebuked. At this time many a church is suffering grievously from the sin of its own members; sin in its ranks.

As I look abroad I am grieved and have great heaviness of spirit at what I see among professing Christians. A very serious matter concerns the amusements engaged in by professing Christians. I see it publicly stated, by some who call themselves Christians, that it is good for Christians to attend the theatre, so that the tone and character of the productions may be improved. The suggestion is about as sensible as if we were bidden to pour a bottle of lavender water into the main sewer to improve its aroma.

If the church is now supposed to raise the tone of the world by imitating it, things have strangely altered since the day when our Lord said, 'Come out from among them . . . and touch not the unclean thing.' Is Heaven to descend to the infernal lake to raise its tone? Such has been the moral condition of the theatre for many a year that it has become too bad for mending. And even if it were mended it would soon become corrupt again. Pass it by with averted gaze, for the house of the strange woman is there.

It has not been my lot ever to enter a theatre during the performance of a play, but I have seen enough when I have come home from journeys at night, while riding past the theatres, to make me pray that our sons and daughters may never go within their doors. It must be a strange school for virtue which attracts the harlot and the debauchee. It is no place for a Christian if it is best appreciated by the irreligious and worldly.

If our church members fall into the habit of frequenting the theatre, we shall soon have them going much further in the direction of vice, and they will lose all relish for the ways of God. If theatre-going became general among professing Christians, it would be the death of piety. Yet one finds the taste for such things increasing on every hand.

Who can suppose amusements surrounded with the seductions of vice to be fit recreation for a pure mind? Who could draw near to God after sitting to admire the performances of the debauched (and I am told that some who have dazzled London society are such)? When behaviour is growing every day more lax and licentious, shall believers lower the standard of their lives? If they do so their spiritual power will depart, and their reason for existence will be over. If there ever could be a time when Christians might relax their rigidity, it surely is not now when the very air is tainted with pollution, and when our streets ring with the newsboys' cries vending filthy publications.

It is profoundly saddening to hear how people talk about acts of sin nowadays; how young men and women without blushing talk of deeds which deprave and destroy, as though they were trifles, or themes for joking. As for those who not only commit lewdness, but who take pleasure in those who do it – 'O my soul, come not thou into their secret.' It will certainly be disastrous for the church of God if her members should become impure. In these days we must be doubly strict, lest any looseness of conduct should come in among us. Actual sin must be repressed with a strong hand, but even the appearance of evil must be avoided.

My dear brethren and sisters, whatever your deficiencies, be pure in heart and lip and life. Never indulge an evil imagination, or speak about things which are unclean. Let them not once be named among you, as becometh saints. A lascivious glance, a doubtful word, a questionable act must be strenuously avoided. Anything and everything that verges upon the unchaste must be rejected.

Only the pure in heart shall see God. We are all subject to human passions, and this wretched flesh of ours is too easily fascinated by those who would pander to its indulgences. In seconds the soul may be led into captivity. Watch unto prayer, especially in these evil days. Cry, 'Lead us not into temptation,' and if the prayer is sincere you will also keep far from doubtful places. Make a covenant with your eyes that you will not look upon that which pollutes, and stop your ears from hearing about it. Watch your lips lest they spread corruption when speaking of sin. I am not afraid that you will step directly into gross sin, but that you may take a very small step on the road that leads to it. Then it will only be a matter of time.

Augustine tells a story of a young friend of his who had the greatest horror of everything connected with the Roman amphitheatre. A heathen friend tried to persuade him to enter the Colosseum, and as he was very hard pressed and was under some obligation to that friend he agreed to go just once, but determined to keep his eyes and ears closed all the time. It would seem to be a very small risk to sit there as one who was blind and deaf, but in the middle of the sports the people so loudly applauded a certain gladiator who had pleased them that he opened his eyes and ears to discover what it was all about. From that moment he was spellbound; he looked on, and enjoyed the sight, and though before he could not bear the very mention of it, he came at last to be a regular frequenter of the cruel sports, and a defender of them, and after a short time he abandoned his profession of Christianity.

Beware of the leaven of worldly pleasure, for its working is silent but sure, and a little of it will leaven the whole lump. Keep up the distinction between a Christian and an unbeliever and make it clearer every day.

Have you heard of the minister who complained to the devil for running off with one of his church members? The fiend replied, 'I found him on my premises, and therefore I claimed him.' I, also, may say, 'Stop!' to the arch-deceiver, but it will be of no use if he finds you on his territory. Every fowler claims the bird which he finds in his own net. This is the argument: 'I caught him in my net, and therefore he is mine.' We shall in vain try to dispute this right of property with the arch-enemy, for possession is nine points of the law. Avoid the appearance of evil. 'But we must not be too rigid,' says one. There is no fear of that in these days. You will never go too far in holiness, nor become too like your Lord Jesus. If anybody accuses you of being too strict and precise, do not grieve but try to deserve the charge. I cannot suppose that at the last great day our Lord Jesus Christ will say to anyone, 'You were not worldly enough. You were too jealous over your conduct, and did not sufficiently conform to the world.' No, my brethren, such a wrong is impossible. He Who said, 'Be ye therefore perfect, even as your Father which is in heaven is perfect,' has set before you a standard beyond which you can never go.

'Well, but,' says one, 'are we to have no enjoyments?' My dear friend, the enjoyments which are prepared for Christians are many and great, but they never include sin and folly. Do you call vice and folly enjoyments?

When I go down into the country I see farmers carrying out great pails of hogwash for the swine, and I never grudge them their dainty meal. I do not protest against their having a full trough twice over. But do I partake with them? Certainly not! I have no taste for that. Do I therefore deny myself? Certainly not! It never struck me that there was anything desirable in their rich mixture. I have no doubt that it has a fine flavour to the creatures for whom it is prepared. It certainly seems to be appreciated.

If worldlings enjoy the pleasures of the world and sin, let them have them, poor souls. They have nothing else to enjoy. They have no paradise for the everlasting future. They have no Christ and Saviour to lean their heads upon. Let them have that which makes them happy while they can be happy. But when I am talking to the children of God I adopt another tone, since for you these things have no charms if you have truly tasted the high delights of fellowship with God.

'But,' you say, 'I would greatly enjoy a little of the pleasures of sin.'

Judge yourselves, then, to be falsely called children of God. 'Whoso-ever is born of God doth not commit sin,' by which is not meant that he does not fall into sin through weakness, but that it is not his desire or plan or delight to commit sin. It is not his way, because he is a new creature, and he finds his joy and pleasure in living as near to God as possible.

'How far may we go in conformity to the world?' is a question that is frequently asked. Have you never heard the story of a lady who wanted a coachman? Two or three called to see her about the post, and, in answer to her enquiries, the first applicant said, 'Yes, madam, you could not have a better coachman than myself.' She replied, 'How near do you think you could drive to danger without an accident?' 'Madam, I could go within a yard of it, and yet you would be perfectly safe.' 'Very well,' she said, 'you will not suit me.'

The second applicant had heard the question upon which the other had been rejected, and therefore he was ready with his answer, 'Danger! madam, why I could drive within a hair's breadth, and yet be perfectly safe.' 'Then you will not suit me at all.' When number three came in, he was asked, 'Are you a good driver?' 'Well,' he replied, 'I am careful and have never met with an accident.' 'But how near do you think you could drive to danger?' 'Madam,' he said, 'that is a thing I never tried; I always drive as far away from danger as ever I can.' The lady at once replied, 'You are the kind of coachman I want, and I will engage you at once.'

Get such a coachman as that yourself to guide your own heart and lead your own character. Do not see how near you can go to sin, but see how far you can keep away from it. If you do not take that advice, and if the Spirit of God does not produce in you purity of life, by and by the church will have to hold up its hands and say, 'Who would have thought it? These were the nice young people of whom so much was expected; these were the good people who used to say, "You must not be too strict," and where are they now?' To avoid the worst keep clear of the bad. As for your Lord's work, be bound to the altar of Christ and be united for ever to Him, and I am sure you will not find that you are losers by giving up worldly pleasures. The Lord's ways are ways of pleasantness, and all His paths are peace. There is a safe and sweet pleasantness in holy living, and the pleasantness lies very much in the fact that an abounding peace springs from it. God grant us grace to keep in these peaceful paths, even though others should call us Puritans and ridicule our holy fear of sin.

8

Counsel for Witnessing Christians
And a word of encouragement

'Then Pharaoh called for Moses and Aaron, and said, Intreat the Lord, that he may take away the frogs from me, and from my people; and I will let the people go, that they may do sacrifice unto the Lord'
(Exodus 8.8).

WHEN IT pleases God by His judgements to humble men He is never at a loss for means. He can use lions or lice, famines or flies. In the armoury of God there are weapons of every kind, from the stars in their courses down to caterpillars in their hosts. The dust of the earth, out of which man is formed, will at God's command leave its dunes and overwhelm a convoy. The waters will forsake their channels, take to the tops of mountains and drown a rebellious race.

When the Lord contends against proud men He has but to lift His finger and countless legions throng around Him, all loyal to their Lord and valiant for His name. Do the proud not know that the beasts of the field are His servants, and the stones of the street obey His bidding? In the case before us, Jehovah has to deal with

Pharaoh, and He humbles him by means of frogs. How strange! How remarkable! One would never have thought that such despicable means would have been used. The Lord began to deal with the proud monarch by turning the waters into blood. But it may be that Pharaoh said in his heart, 'What a great man I must be for Jehovah to find it necessary to work a terrible miracle in order to conquer me.' Perhaps he went on his way unhumbled.

This time the Lord will deal with him in another manner. The croaking frogs which came up from all the banks of the Nile marched up in countless hordes from every reservoir and marsh, entering into his chamber and coming upon his bed. He could neither sleep nor eat nor walk abroad without encountering the loathsome reptiles. The Lord seemed by this to say, 'Who are you that I should do great things to conquer you? I will even vanquish you by frogs.'

It was doubly appropriate for God to choose frogs to humble Egypt's king, because frogs were worshipped by that nation as emblems of the deity. Images of a certain frog-headed goddess were placed in the catacombs, and frogs themselves were preserved with sacred honours. These be your gods, O Egypt! You shall have more than enough of them!

The Lord has sure ways of reaching the hearts of proud men. He knows how to reach the rich, and make them sit begging. He can soon place the strong and healthy among the invalids. His arrows can pierce through a sevenfold harness of steel. No person is so protected as to be beyond the reach of the Almighty.

In drawing lessons from Pharaoh's plight, I will begin by noting that – in times of sore trouble ungodly people *find the servants of the Lord are of great value.* 'Then Pharaoh called for Moses and Aaron.' On account of the frogs he longs to see the ministers of the Lord. How is this? The man was brought to his senses, and when this happens, people value those whom they previously despised.

Listen to this story. There came a man of God to Bethel, where King Jeroboam was setting up the golden calves, and he began to cry against the altar. Then Jeroboam stretched forth his hand, and cried, 'Lay hold on him.' In a moment the rebel's right arm withered, and hung by his side useless. Then he turned to the man of God, whom he was about to arrest, and said, 'Intreat the Lord for me.' Persecutors have often been forced to crouch at the feet of those whom they would have destroyed.

Another story will set forth the same truth. King Saul had been forsaken of God, and the Philistines pressed hard upon him. In his extremity he resorted to a woman who professed to deal with the spirits of the dead. With whom would he speak? He cries, 'Bring me up Samuel.' Samuel was the man who had most sternly rebuked him. One would have thought that Samuel was the last person he would wish to see; but in his need he asks for no one else.

When ungodly men get into real troubles, they do not say, 'Bring me up the jolly fellow who drank with me.' In their tribulation they think not of such. They do not cry, 'Bring me up the person with whom I sported in sin, that I may again enjoy that person's company.' In their distress they desire better advisers. They may say, 'Oh, for an hour with the man of God whom once I scorned!' It is the old tale repeated – Pharaoh, when his troubles were multiplied, calls for Moses and Aaron!

This is also to be accounted for by the fact that God puts a mysterious honour upon His faithful servants. The painters place haloes about the heads of Bible saints. There were no such crowns of light upon them literally, and yet within the portrayal there lies a great truth. He who leads an upright, holy, gracious life has a power about him which impresses the beholder. Pharaoh had said, 'Get you unto your burdens,' addressing Moses and Aaron as if they were slaves; but now he sends for them, and pleads for their prayers on his behalf.

A poor saint was laid at a rich man's door, full of sores. He begged for the crumbs that fell from the rich man's table. 'Moreover the dogs came and licked his sores.' The rich man, clothed with purple and fine linen, took small note of this saint of God; but what a change happened on a day when the beggar died, and was carried by angels into Abraham's bosom, and the rich man also died, and was buried! In hell the rich man lifted up his eyes, and Lazarus had honour. He begged that Lazarus might be sent to cool his burning tongue with the tip of his finger dipped in water. They had changed places, for God had crowned His poor servant with glory and honour. The halo was around the head of Lazarus.

This honour is undoubtedly set on believers that they may be of service to ungodly people. God intends, by their means, to bless the penitent. When it was wheat harvest, and a thunderstorm came because Israel desired a king, you remember that, while the artillery of God was heard, the people trembled, and besought Samuel the prophet to pray for them. He said, 'God forbid that I should sin against the Lord in ceasing to pray for you.' Godly Samuel's prayer was heard for them.

Much later on, an earthquake shook the foundations of a prison, and loosed the bands of the prisoners. Then the gaoler woke up terrified that his prisoners had escaped, and that he should have to die for it. But there stood Paul, the man whom he had thrust into the inner prison, and whose feet he had made fast in the stocks. The gaoler, trembling before him, cried out, 'Sirs, what must I do to be saved?' The answer was given; he was directed to believe and to be baptised, and the gaoler and his house were saved.

If God's servants are treated with scorn and harshness they need not fear, for they are put just where they are that unconverted men may be blessed by their agency. It is clear that in times of trouble godly men and women are at a premium.

Secondly, in times of sore trial ungodly people *find prayer to be valuable.* Then Pharaoh called for Moses and Aaron, and said, 'Intreat the Lord.' Pharaoh begs an interest in the prayers of good men: this is a fine change since the day wherein he said, 'Who is the Lord that I should obey his voice?'

When people are sick and near to die, they send for us to pray with them. That old philosopher, Bion, showed much wisdom in his biting sarcasm. He was on a ship, and found that among the passengers there were foul-mouthed desperadoes. While they were venting all manner of abominations a storm came on, and they began to pray. Then Bion cried out to them, 'Hold your tongues, for if the gods only know that *you* are here they will sink the vessel. Be quiet, lest your prayers should be our ruin.' One's thoughts have run along these lines when we have seen men fulfilling the old adage –

> *When the devil was sick,*
> *The devil a saint would be.*

Why is it that reprobates take to praying when they are in deep trouble? Frequently, *superstition moves them.* They regard a prayer as a spell or magical charm. So in their folly they send for a minister, and cry, 'Intreat the Lord for me.'

In certain instances an ungodly person's sudden hope in prayer is the result of a *condemning faith.* 'What?' you say. 'Does faith ever condemn people?' Yes. When people have faith enough to know that there is a God Who sends judgements upon them, and that nothing can remove those judgements but the hand that sent them. There are people who yet never pray themselves, but cry to friends, 'Intreat the Lord for me.' There is a measure of faith which goes to increase a person's condemnation, since he ought to know that if what he believes is true, then the proper thing is to pray himself.

It would have been a wonderfully good sign if Pharaoh had said, 'Join with me, O Moses and Aaron, while I pray unto Jehovah that He may take the frogs from me.' But, no, he had only a condemning faith, which contented itself with other men's prayers.

In many instances this desire for prayer is *one of the movements of the Spirit upon the heart of man.* When a poor, afflicted man, in the depth of poverty, struck with consumption, or laid aside by some other deadly disease, desires that a minister would come and pray with him, we will never treat such a wish with neglect. While it is our duty to expose the superstition which often lurks beneath the wish, we also hope that some good thing towards the Lord may be in it. It is, perhaps, the prodigal saying, 'I will arise, and go unto my Father, and I will inquire the way home.' I hope it is so.

Thirdly, in times of great troubles the ungodly *often pray wrongly.* The petitions which people offer when they are in distress are often wrong prayers. Pharaoh said – 'Intreat the Lord, that he may take away the frogs from me.' A fatal flaw is manifest in that prayer. *It contains no confession of sin.* He does not say, 'I have rebelled against the Lord; intreat that I may find forgiveness!' He loves sin as much as ever. A prayer without penitence is a prayer without acceptance. If no tear has fallen upon it, it is withered. You must come to God as a sinner through a Saviour, but by no other way. He that comes to God like the Pharisee, with, 'God, I thank thee, that I am not as other men are,' never draws near to God at all; but he that cries, 'God be merciful to me a sinner,' has come to God by the way which God has Himself appointed.

Pharaoh's prayer *dealt only with the punishment*: 'Take away the frogs; take away the frogs; take away the frogs.' That is his one cry. So we hear the sick exclaim, 'Pray that I may get well.' The drunkard begs that he may be helped out of his poverty. The impenitent sinner cries, 'Pray that my child may not be taken from me.'

It is not wrong to pray, 'Take away the frogs.' The evil is that this was the whole of his prayer. He said not, 'Take away my sins,' but, 'Take away the frogs.' He did not cry, 'Lord, take away my heart of stone,' but only, 'Take away the frogs.' The Lord did hear his petition, but nothing came of it. The frogs were gone, but flies came directly after, and all sorts of plagues followed in rapid succession, and his heart was hardened still.

When Cain had murdered his brother did he express a regret? No. He only murmured, 'My punishment is greater than I can bear.' Esau sold his birthright. Did he repent of the sin of having been a profane person, and seek pardon carefully? Not he; but he sought carefully with tears to get back his birthright, and he found no place for repentance in his father Isaac; the blessing had gone to Jacob, and on Jacob it must remain.

Another telling case is that of Simon Magus. When Peter told him that he was in the gall of bitterness and in the bond of iniquity he replied, 'Pray ye to the Lord for me, that none of these things which ye have spoken come upon me;' that was all he cared about. He expressed no desire to be delivered from his evil way, but only to be screened from the consequences of it.

Fourthly, in times of sore troubles the ungodly are *apt to make great promises.* Pharaoh cried, 'Take away the frogs . . . and I will let the people go, that they may do sacrifice unto the Lord.' In this way people have talked when they were down with fever, or when they were in some alarming situation. They have said, 'Please God I escape this once, I will be a very different man.' Such promises are *generally boastful.* Notice here the proud language of Pharaoh. 'I will let the people go.' (We must place the emphasis on the 'I'.) He is a great king, and he gives his royal word. 'I will let the people go.'

Some folks are very big when they promise God, 'I will do this, and I will do that.' But they cannot. They say that they are going to have a new heart and a right spirit. Are they looking to create it in themselves? True conversion does not begin by talking of what 'I' will do. It begins in casting ourselves upon the Lord, and begging Him to work all our works in us.

Pharaoh's promises were *all a lie.* I dare say that for the moment he meant them; but he did not keep his word, for he did not let the people go. 'When Pharaoh saw that there was respite, he hardened his heart, and hearkened not unto them; as the Lord had said.' Has not that been the case with many others? They promised 'faithfully', but it was not so. God says to them, 'Thou hast not lied unto men, but unto God.'

Mark well that, in all this, Pharaoh *increased his guilt*. His vows heaped up his transgressions. He forgot his promises; but God did not. They were laid by in store against him, and the blows of God upon him fell heavier and heavier, until at last Jehovah drowned him and his chosen captains in the Red Sea.

I will tell you how God deals with His own children. A certain man, to all appearance, feared God with a sincere heart. He was once an earnest Christian, a member of the church, and a worker in its service, faithful to his light, and fervent in spirit. But he grew cold. He had a farm, and it occupied nearly all his time. He was filled with an intense desire to grow rich, and therefore he devoted his attention to his business till he grew colder and colder in divine things, and the means of grace on weekdays were forsaken.

Work for God was dropped, communion with God ceased, and he became to all appearance an utter worldling. But yet he was a child of God, and this is how his Father restored him. He took from him the wife of his youth to whom his heart was knit. But this made him more worldly than before, because his wife had been a great help to him in the farm, and now she was gone he must stick to it more than ever. Nothing came of the first chastisement except increased sin. He had only one son, for whom he was saving up his money, and working his business, but he saw his son cut down with consumption, like his mother. This also made him still more worldly. It ought to have brought him to his knees, but it did not.

He carried on the practice of prayer, but with little heart. He said, 'Now my dear son, who was such a comfort to me, has gone, I can hardly get out on Sundays at all. I *must* look after the cows and attend to the stock.' So he sank deeper in the mire.

Then the Lord began to deal with him in another way. He had a bad season, and his farm lost money, careful as he was. Next year was worse, and cattle plague emptied his stalls. He was brought down to poverty and could barely keep at the farm, for the rent ran behind. Still he did not yield. He had tender moments now and then, but he was usually hard, for he now felt that God was dealing severely with him. He felt angry against God, stuck to his business more than ever, and the things of God were forgotten.

Then the Lord took his erring child more closely to hand than before, and sent him an incurable disease. The worldly farmer lay upon a sick-bed worrying. He did not turn to the Lord even then.

Last of all, his house caught fire, and as the barn, ricks, and house were ablaze, they carried him out into the open air upon the bed from which he could not stir, and he was heard to say, 'Blessed be the Lord! Blessed be the Lord! I am cured at last.' Nothing would cure him till everything was gone from him. Was not that a pity? He was saved so as by fire. He would be 'as the horse, or as the mule, which have no understanding: whose mouth must be held in with bit and bridle,' and therefore he had to suffer for it. I pray you do not copy him.

People of God, do not make rods for your own backs in that way. Do not drive your heavenly Father to hard measures. If He means to bless you He will not let you go unpunished; but He will smite you with heavy strokes. I remember one who used to bless God for a broken leg. He said that he never ran in the ways of God until he was lame. I believe that some parents never loved the heavenly Father till their dear infant child was taken away. The Shepherd tried to get the mother sheep into the fold, but she would not come; so He took up her lamb and carried it away in His arms, and then the mother followed Him.

It may be that a reader has suffered many a loss, as if – 'You have been smitten till your whole head is sick and your whole heart faint.' Will you not turn unto your God without more ado? His blows are sent in mercy: it is better far that you should have a hell here than a hell hereafter. It is better for you to live a lifelong agony than to be cast into hell for ever. The Lord Jesus Christ died for guilty, wilful sinners, and if they look to Him, they shall at once be forgiven.

(Edited from a sermonette entitled, 'Take Away the Frogs' in *The Sword & the Trowel*, 1884, not included in the *Metropolitan Tabernacle Pulpit*.)

9

The Sparrow and the Swallow
Safety for seeking souls

'Yea, the sparrow hath found an house, and the swallow a nest for herself, where she
may lay her young, even thine altars, O Lord of hosts, my King, and my God'
(Psalm 84.3).

WHEN DAVID was far away from the services of the tabernacle he envied the birds that had built their nests near the sacred shrine. It seems that these birds had found two things: firstly houses for themselves, and secondly nests for their young. Both these things Christians find in Christ, and also, in a sense, in congregations of believers gathered for public worship.

Our first question shall be, *What were those creatures that found a house?* Well, they were only sparrows, yet they found a house near the altars of God, and therefore David envied them. Sparrows are *very insignificant* things. 'Are not five sparrows sold for two farthings?' said Christ to His disciples.

You and I, dear friends, when we really see ourselves as we are in God's sight, because of our sin, feel even more insignificant than sparrows, and realise that to be blotted out of the universe would be a gain rather than a loss. What unworthy creatures we see ourselves to be, once God pours upon us the bright light of His Word!

Then we think that any mercy is far too good for us to receive. Yet, as the sparrows were permitted to find their house under the eaves of God's tabernacle, so we, worthless as we are, may come and build under the shelter of His great house of mercy. There we may find a safe refuge and a perfect security for all time, and for all eternity.

You who think yourself despised and forgotten, remember that the sparrow has found a house on God's altar. Come, then, and see if there is not space there also for you! Jesus said, 'Him that cometh to me I will in no wise cast out;' and the apostle Paul says, 'God hath chosen the foolish things of the world to confound the wise; and God hath chosen the . . . base things of the world, and things which are despised . . .' Therefore, though you feel yourself to be a nobody, come to the Saviour with confidence, for He will not reject you.

The sparrows were not only very insignificant, they were also *very needy*. They needed a house, a place of shelter, and they found it at God's altar. How needy also are we! Though we are insignificant, our wants are anything but insignificant. How much we need! Were it not for God's superabounding mercy, we should all be in hell. Were it not for His unspeakable goodness, we should this day have no hope of grace, no prospect of pardon, no assurance of a holy, happy Heaven hereafter.

Our wants are countless, and every moment brings a fresh one, and all the supplies of the past and the present are not sufficient to meet the voracious demands that will come upon us in the future. The sparrow, needy creature that she was, having nothing to bring to God's house, found there a place freely given to her; and, in our case, the infinite supply of divine mercy, in the Person of the Lord Jesus Christ, is freely given to us.

You need not bring anything with you when you come to Christ, only come and trust Him, but come, flying with the wings of faith, to find a house and a home in Him. At the great altar where Christ was offered as the one sacrifice for sin for ever, the most needy soul that ever lived on the face of the earth will find a welcome.

These sparrows were *uninvited guests*, yet they found a house and took possession of it, and they were never criticised for doing so. But, my dear hearers, you who have never come to the Lord Jesus Christ are *not* uninvited guests. The Gospel invitation rings through this building every Sabbath day –

> *Come and welcome,*
> *Come to Jesus, sinner come!*

We not only invite you, but we earnestly press you, in Christ's name, to come and put your trust in His great sacrifice, assuring you that if you do so you shall find an everlasting and blessed home for your souls. The sparrows were bold enough to find a house when no one told them to do so; so will you not be bold enough, fearful though you may be, to take the divine mercy freely proffered to you?

The Lord delights to have great things thought of Him; and if you will only think great things of His love and mercy, I will warrant you that you will never think thoughts that shall outstrip the reality. Let us learn, then, from the sparrow finding her house near to God's altar, that although we are inconsiderable and insignificant, although we are full of needs, and although we may even deem ourselves to be uninvited, yet we are at liberty to come to the Saviour, and find in Him our eternal dwelling-place.

Next, what does the text tell us that these sparrows did? The text says, 'Yea, the sparrow hath *found* an house.' Clearly, then, *she looked for it*. The sparrow wanted a house, and she searched to see where she could find it. One reason why many do not find salvation is because they do not look for it. Many of them do not even know that they need it, or, if they know it as a matter of doctrine, they do not believe it enough to look for it, and appropriate it as their own.

I am persuaded that no one ever sincerely sought salvation through Jesus Christ, without finding it. I do not believe that among all the lost there is one who will be able to tell the Lord that he honestly and earnestly sought His mercy, yet could not obtain it. If you have not found Christ, my dear hearer, it is because you have not sought Him, for He said, 'He that seeketh findeth; and to him that knocketh it shall be opened.' I grant you that the blessing may be delayed for a while. You may be some time in finding peace, perhaps through your ignorance, or through some cherished sin that you have not given up; but if you truly come to the throne of grace, and cry in earnest for mercy, as surely as God is in Christ Jesus, He will stretch out His sceptre toward you, and you shall find grace in His sight. Be encouraged to persevere in your search after salvation, and ask that the help of the Holy Spirit may be given to you.

Notice that a suitable house existed for the sparrow, or she could never have found it. A traveller in Palestine writes in his journal that, as he was wandering among the ruins on the site of the Temple at Jerusalem, he noticed a little bird – known in the Hebrew as *tzippor*, or sparrow – fly out of a crevice between two great stones where the mortar or cement had been removed, and he thought at once of these words, 'The sparrow hath found an house.'

That is just what David meant. The sparrow no doubt found a little vacant place, just what she wanted, and in she went, and there was her 'house' ready made for her. Let me say to you who seek rest in Christ, there is rest prepared for you! He Who has prepared your heart to seek Him has prepared that which you long to find. It is not for you to make a salvation for yourself. Your salvation is accomplished and you only have to find it. It is not for you to make an atonement for yourself; atonement for sin has been made, once for all, on Calvary. It is not for you to make righteousness for yourself; the righteousness that Christ Jesus wrought is perfect, and you cannot add any of your own.

As Bunyan said, 'Does not your mouth water as you hear this? Do you not say, "Is all this really prepared for me? Then, why do I not have it?"' Why not indeed? In my Master's name, I do assure you that 'all things are ready' for all who will seek Him, for every soul that will trust Him.

'Yea, the sparrow hath found an house.' This also shows that when she had discovered it, *she appropriated it.* There was the little place, so snug and cosy, just on the warm side of the tabernacle, where the south wind would blow and she would be shielded from the cold, and in went the little bird. She had found it, and she took care to make it her own by personal appropriation.

Now, we may find Christ, in a sense, so as to know much about Him, yet not truly to find Him. The root of the matter is to get Christ for yourself, and in this respect you must be selfish, and you can thus be selfish without being sinful. You must personally lay hold of Christ if you would be saved.

Someone set out to teach a little girl this lesson when the child was waiting upon him while he was ill. 'Please pour out my medicine, Jane,' said the sick man; and when it was poured out, he said, 'Now, take it for me.' 'O!' she said, 'I would willingly do it, but the medicine would not do you any good if I took it.' 'Exactly,' said he, 'and as I must personally take the medicine before it can do me good, you must personally believe in the Lord Jesus Christ, because another person's faith can do you no good.'

Faith is a personal thing. You must repent for yourself, believe for yourself, and lay hold on Christ for yourself. It would have been no benefit to that little bird if all other sparrows had found houses for themselves and she had remained shelterless in the storm. She must take a house for herself.

What exactly did the sparrow find in her house? The word *house* is a simple one, but it says much. When we find a house for our souls in the Lord Jesus Christ, *we find safety in Him,* even as the sparrow found safety in her house. When the stormy wind blew around her, she felt safe in her stone fortress by the altar, and when the storm of conscience beats upon us, we feel safe in our hiding-place where Jesus Christ suffered for us.

And when the last dreadful storm of divine judgement shall come, we shall be safe beneath the shelter of the atonement that He offered upon Calvary. When the earth and all its works are burned up, and the heavens shall pass away with a great noise, no hurt shall come to the man to whom Christ is 'an hiding place from the wind, and a covert from the tempest'. Next to safety, we find in Christ rest.

> *'Tis done! the great transaction's done;*
> *I am my Lord's, and He is mine.*

My salvation is finished, my sins are pardoned, my security is established by the promise and oath of God Himself, and ratified by the blood of the everlasting covenant. If this is your happy condition, you can enjoy the blissful composure of those beloved by the Lord, 'and the peace of God, which passeth all understanding, shall keep your hearts and minds through Christ Jesus.' Just as the sparrow felt perfectly at rest when she had entered her house, so we enjoy complete, absolute, unbroken rest when we have truly believed in our Lord and Saviour Jesus Christ. 'Thou wilt keep him in perfect peace, whose mind is stayed on thee: because he trusteth in thee.'

Further a house is *a place of abode*. The sparrow lived in her house, and whoever finds the Lord Jesus Christ lives in Him. He has heard his Master's blessed command, 'Abide in me,' and he desires to dwell there. Brothers and sisters in Christ, we have not a mere temporary lodging-place, out of which we may some day be driven back into the cold world where we used to live. That would be a poor prospect for us, but we can say with Moses, 'Lord, thou hast been our dwelling place in all generations.'

A house is also *a place of delight.* When a man reaches his home, he is at his ease, and can be happy. The sparrow, when she reaches her home, is perfectly content. Her wants are supplied, and she chirps her evening song of joy. So, when we make our home in Christ, our soul is filled with delight. But the point upon which the psalmist seemed to lay the greatest emphasis was that *the sparrow's house was near to God's earthly dwelling place*; and when we abide in Christ, how near we are to God! No nearness imaginable can be greater than Christ's nearness to His Father, and if we are in Him we are, in His Person, as near even as He is!

A further meaning which may be found in our text is that believers, *like the sparrow, find a house in the assemblies of the saints.* Cultivate more and more your love for the assemblies of the saints. We have no reverence for bricks and mortar, for we do not believe in the sanctity of any one place above others. But we have love and reverence for the living temple of God, built up of living men and women whose hearts are sanctified by the Holy Spirit, and we can say of these assemblies –

> *I have been there, and still will go,*
> *'Tis like a little Heaven below.*

And we can also say –

> *My tongue repeats her vows,*
> *'Peace to this sacred house!'*
> *For there my friends and kindred dwell;*
> *And, since my glorious God*
> *Makes thee His blest abode,*
> *My soul shall ever love thee well.*

There are many people here who scarcely ever have any peace except when they are sitting in this house of prayer, and who find here the richest enjoyments they ever know. I know some of God's afflicted children, who have but little sacred happiness except when the holy hymn goes up in glorious peals to Heaven, and they can join in it –

Then they forget their pains a while,
And in the pleasure lose the smart.

The second main point in our text concerns the swallow. After a person is saved, that person's first anxiety, if a parent, will be for the children. We read – 'The swallow *[hath found]* a nest for herself, where she may lay her young, even thine altars, O Lord of hosts, my King, and my God.' Every Christian should long for the good of the children, and the person who does not labour and pray for the salvation of his own offspring has reason to doubt whether he knows the grace of God himself. The assemblies of believers should be a nest for little ones also.

First, *the young are safe there.* In the Sabbath School they will be safe. Your children will be like the swallows in this respect, *they will be pretty sure to return to the nest even if they do leave it for a while.* Though the swallows may fly over the sea to far-away lands, yet when the next season comes they find their way back again to the old nest and home. Though some of our sons and daughters may grow up and leave the house of God for a while, they cannot altogether forget it. The recollection of their father's prayers and their mother's tears will follow them wherever they roam.

Refrain your eyes from weeping, mothers: your sons and daughters shall come back again. Possibly, when you sleep beneath the clod they will remember what they heard as children. Words forgotten for fifty years may yet ring in their souls, and lead to their eternal salvation. In the meantime, associate them as far as you can with all that is going on in their former nest or church, so that they shall feel at home when they return.

How can we lay our children before Christ, as the swallow laid her young before God's altar? I answer, first, *by prayer.* The Lord will hear our prayers for our children. *Example* will also help toward the end we have in view – a godly example at home. And *personal instruction* will also help. We must talk to our children, one by one, alone, about their souls.

Resolve that, if your children perish, it shall not be through any fault of yours. Brethren and sisters, if you are like the sparrow, and have found a house, now be like the swallow, and find not only a nest for yourself, but a place where you may lay your young, even God's altar upon which Christ offered His great atoning sacrifice.

I wonder what other birds are represented here in this congregation? I fear that I am addressing some who will not heed what I have been saying. They are not like the sparrow and the swallow but they are like the eagle, that was far too ambitious to think of building her nest anywhere near God's altar. The eagle was too fond of soaring and struggling, too fond of high and lofty things. But there will come a time when the pride of man shall be laid low.

Possibly there is one here who is like the vulture, far too foul to think of building in God's house, fond of everything that is unclean, and of sinful amusements and pleasures. The time will come when sin will be as bitter to you as now it is sweet, and far more so, for it 'will eat as doth a canker'. Or perhaps there is one here who is like the cormorant, who will not build on God's house because he is far too greedy for gold and to amass property. Have you never heard of the rich fool whose soul was required of him the very night on which he boasted of his wealth?

If you do not care for your own soul, it must seem irrelevant for me to talk to you about your children. Yet I will say to any unconverted person here that it will increase your misery intolerably to see your children lost through your example. May you be saved yourself, with your children, in the spirit of the text – 'The swallow *[hath found]* a nest for herself, where she may lay her young, even thine altars, O Lord of hosts, my King, and my God.'

10

Is the Lord With Us?
A call to attend the prayer meeting

'And the inhabitants of one city shall go to another, saying, Let us go speedily to pray
before the Lord, and to seek the Lord of hosts: I will go also'
(Zechariah 8.21).

O NE OF THE first signs of God's presence among a people
is that they take great interest in divine worship, as they
did in our text. It is clear that they no longer regard divine
worship as wearying, but begin to value the means of grace, and
make good use of them. The first solemn assembly mentioned here
is the prayer meeting, and the first cry of the people is, 'Let us go
speedily to pray.' From long observation I may assert that the condition of a church may be accurately gauged by its prayer meetings.

If the spirit of prayer is not with the people, the minister may
preach like an angel but cannot expect success. There may be in that
church wealth, talent, labour, and many outreach efforts, but the
Lord is not there. Prayer is as sure evidence of the presence of God
as the rising of the thermometer is evidence of an increase in tem-
perature. If God is near a church it must pray. If He is not there, one

of the obvious signs of His absence will be lethargy in prayer.

When God's people pray it is clear that they have a sense of their needs, feeling that they need the help that only God can give them. They feel their need of His help if sinners are to be converted, and their need of His help if those who are saved are to be steadfast and grow in grace. He who never prays does not know his own needs.

Also, the love which God's people have for prayer shows their desire after heavenly things. Those who frequently meet together for importunate, wrestling prayer demonstrate that they long to see the Lord's kingdom come. They are not so taken up with their own business that they cannot afford time to think of God's business. They are not so occupied with the world's pleasures that they take no pleasure in the things of God.

Church members who never pray for the good of the church, have no love for it. If they do not plead for sinners they have no love for the Saviour. How can they be truly converted persons? Those who constantly forsake meetings for prayer may well suspect the genuineness of their conversion. I am not, of course, alluding to those who are barred by circumstances, but those who, by trivial causes, absent themselves from prayer meetings. Are they not dead branches of the vine? May they not expect to be taken away before long?

Meetings for prayer also reveal the level of our belief in the living God as One Who hears prayer. People will not continue in supplication if they do not believe that God hears them. Who would persevere in a vain exercise? Our united prayers prove that we know that God is, and that He is a rewarder of them that diligently seek Him. We know that the Lord is able to work according to our desires, and that He is willing to be entreated of us.

I have never known a man who needed money, and had a good trade, who would not exercise his trade. Equally, I have never known a man who believed that prayer was effectual, who did not engage in prayer. It is a bad sign for any community of Christians when prayer is at a low ebb, for it is clear that they do not believe that God will enrich them in answer to their petitions.

Our own meetings for prayer have excited general astonishment by the numbers attending, but they are not all they might be. I shall lay it on the conscience of each one to ask whether you are as prayerful as you should be.

Do you know of a church member who has not attended a prayer meeting for a month? Do you know of church members who never assemble even once in a quarter? Do you know of any who have not been to the prayer meeting in this place for the last six months? Do you know such? I will do no more than hint that such people may exist, but if you know them, will you give them my Christian love, and say that nothing depresses the pastor's spirit like the absence of church members from the public assemblies for prayer, and that if anything could make him strong in the Lord and give him courage to go forward in the Lord's work, it would be if all of you were to make the prayer meeting your special delight. I shall be satisfied when I see our prayer meetings as crowded as the services for preaching. A vastly larger amount of prayer ought to be among us than at present, and if the Lord visits us He will set us praying without ceasing.

But next, the people of our text also took an interest in meetings for instruction. I find that the Chaldee translates the second sentence, 'Let us seek the doctrine of Jehovah of hosts.' God sends impulses of enquiry over people's minds, and suddenly places of worship which were half empty become crowded. Preachers also become quickened, and speak with earnestness and life. During the revival under John the Baptist, the people went in crowds into the wilderness to hear the strange preacher who bade them repent.

The revival under the apostles was marked by their preaching the Word everywhere, and the people listening. This was the great token of the Reformation. Meetings were held under Gospel Oaks, out on the commons and away in lone houses. Also in glens and woods people thronged to listen to the Word of God.

This also marked the last grand revival of religion in our country under Whitefield and Wesley. The Word of the Lord was precious in those days, and whether the Gospel was preached among the colliers of Kingswood, or the rabble of Kennington Common, tens of thousands were awakened, and rejoiced in the joyful notes of free grace.

They said one to another, 'Let us seek the Lord.' It is recorded that Moorfields would be full of light on a dark winter's morning at five o'clock when Mr Whitefield was to preach, because so many people would be finding their way, each one carrying a lantern. It was the same in Zoar Street, Southwark, when John Bunyan was out of prison and was going to preach. A couple of thousand would assemble at five o'clock in the morning to enjoy his testimony.

John Foxe speaks of when the Reformation was breaking out, in this vein: 'It was lovely to see their travels, earnest seekings, burning zeal, Bible readings, watchings, sweet assemblies, resort of one neighbour to another for conference and mutual confirmation.' He adds, 'All which may make us now to blush for shame in these our days of free profession.' We may take for ourselves the good man's hint, and feel shame for neglected opportunities, cold devotions, and disregard of the Word of God.

Our fathers loved to meet for prayer, and to hear the preaching of the Truth; and when they came together it was with an intensely earnest desire to obtain the divine blessing. To get it they risked life and liberty, meeting even when fine and imprisonment or perhaps the gallows might be their reward. We long for such earnestness for ourselves. May the Lord Jesus send it to us by the working of His Holy Spirit.

It is a great and sure sign of God visiting His people when *they stir each other up* to attend upon the means of grace. 'The inhabitants of one city shall go to another, saying, Let us go speedily to pray before the Lord.' They did not merely ask one another to go as they casually met, but purposely went to others in order to exhort. They made a journey specifically to do this. They had such a desire that greater numbers might come together to worship that they took much trouble. God will be with us if each one shall be anxious to bring others. The ways of Zion do mourn and languish when few assemble for prayer. We feel like sparrows alone on the house-top when this is the case.

In our text, there does not appear to have been any minister or missionary employed to go from one city to another saying, 'Let us go and pray.' The people themselves understood the duty of invitation and persuasion, and said, 'Let *us* go and pray before the Lord.' The people themselves attended to mutual provocation to love and to good works. How I wish they did so now, and that the hearts of the people were so warm that they would do it spontaneously among themselves. My brethren, may you thus be pastors to one another.

There are far too many of you for me to look after personally, therefore I pray you be stirrers of one another up to every good word and work. I believe that when a person stirs others up it is good for himself. This morning I ask you to visit one another, and to say, 'Come, let us not as a church lose the presence of God after nearly twenty years' enjoyment of it: let not our minister's hands grow weak by our neglect of prayer; let not the work of the church flag through our indifference; but let us make a brotherly covenant that we will go speedily to pray before the Lord and seek the Lord of hosts, that we may retain His presence and have yet more of it, to the praise of the glory of His grace.'

I must pass on to notice that in our text it is a sure mark of God's visiting a people, when *they are urgent to* attend upon these holy meetings *at once*. The text says, 'Let us go *speedily* to pray.' This means, I suppose, that when the time came to pray, they were punctual. They were not laggards, coming into the assembly unnecessarily late.

I wish late-comers would remember David's choice. You will remember the part he wished to take in the house of God, as a door-keeper. Door-keepers are the first in and the last out, and David wished to be first at the service, and the last to leave. It has been said that Dissenters in years gone by placed a clock outside the meeting-house so that they might never enter late, but the modern chapels place the clock inside, so that their preachers may not keep them too long. Let us never keep Jesus Christ waiting, for He is sure to be punctual, even if only two or three are met together in His name.

The expression, however, means more than this. 'Let us go speedily' means, let us go *heartily*. Do not let us crawl to prayer, but let us go to it as people who have an activity before them which attracts them. When the angels serve God they never do it as though they were half asleep. They are alive and burning like flames of fire. They have six wings, and no doubt use them all. When the Lord saith, 'Gabriel, go upon My bidding,' he outstrips the lightning. If only we could exhibit such ardour and zest in prayer to God! When we pray, let us pray as if we meant it. When we worship, let us worship with all our hearts.

The words, 'Let us go speedily', mean – let us go instantly. If any good thing has been neglected, and we resolve to attend to it better, let us do it at once. When is the best time to repent of sin? Today. When is the best time for a cold heart to grow warm? Today. When is the season for a sluggish Christian to be industrious? Today. When is the period for a backslider to return? Today. When is the time for one who has crawled along the road to Heaven to mend his pace? Today.

Is it not always today? Tomorrow is only in the fool's almanac: it exists nowhere else. I beseech the church of God in this place to be yet more alive. Time is flying – we cannot afford to lose it. The devil is wide awake, why should we be asleep? Error is stalking through the land. Evil influences are abroad everywhere. People are dying, hell is filling, the grave is gorged and yet is insatiable, and the maw of destruction is not yet satisfied. Awake, arise, Christians!

I know we are all apt to think that we live in the most important era of history; and I admit that under certain aspects every day is a crisis, but I claim liberty to say that there never was a period in the world's history when Christian activity, and prayerfulness, and genuine revival were more needed than just now.

Where is our nation? Does it not seem as if the people had gone mad on their idols? Do you not see everywhere the old orthodox faith forsaken, and men occupying Christian pulpits who do not believe, and who even denounce the doctrines which they have sworn to defend? Might I not say of Christendom in England, that 'the whole head is sick, and the whole heart faint'? Her Nazarites were purer than snow, and their separation from the world was known of all men, but now they are defiled with worldliness.

From the daughter of Zion her beauty is departed. Thus saith the Lord, 'Arise, cry out in the night . . . pour out thine heart like water before the face of the Lord,' and then the Lord will return and be gracious to His inheritance.

When God visits a people they not only attend to prayer and preaching, but they specifically go to 'seek the Lord of hosts'. It is so easy to fall into formal worship. 'I have been to the prayer meeting. I have done my duty, and I can go home satisfied. I have taken a seat at the Tabernacle and listened to two sermons on the Sunday, and I feel I have done my duty.' What a poor way of living! We must want a great deal more than that. At the prayer meeting I must see God. I must pour out my soul before Him. I must feel that the spirit of prayer has been there, and that I have participated in it, otherwise, what was the good of my being there?

I must, when in the assembly on the Lord's Day, find some blessing to my own soul. I must get another glimpse of the Saviour. I
must come to be somewhat more like Him. I must feel my sin
rebuked, or my flagging graces revived. I must feel that God has
been blessing poor sinners and bringing them to Christ. I must feel,
indeed, that I have come into contact with God, or else what is my
Sunday worth? If God shall bless you, you will only count as true
worship that which is of the spirit, the heart, and the soul.

It is a certain sign of God's visiting a people when *each one of them*
is resolved for himself to wait upon God in a spiritual manner.
Notice the last four words of the text: 'I will go also.' Not one ruled
himself out. It is said of Julius Caesar that he owed his victories to
the fact that he never said to his soldiers, 'Go,' but always said, 'Let
us go.' Example is mightier than precept.

Poor Latimer spoke bravely when he was to be burnt with Ridley,
a younger and stronger man. As Ridley walked to the stake, Latimer,
quaint to the last, cried to his brother, 'Have after, as fast as my poor
old legs can carry me.' The dear saint was going to his burning as
fast as he could; not at all hesitant to lay his aged body upon the
altar for his Lord. That is the kind of person who makes others excel.

I should like to put this very personally to all the members of this
church. We have enjoyed the presence and blessing of God for many
years in a very remarkable manner, and it has not been taken from
us. However, I am jealous, I believe with godly jealousy and not
unbelief, lest there should be among us a slackness in prayer, a lack
of zeal for the glory of God, and a neglect of the souls of our neighbours. Let each one say within himself, 'I will go also. The church
shall be the subject of *my* prayer. The minister shall share in my
petitions. The Sunday School shall not be forgotten. The College
shall be remembered in supplication. The Orphanage shall have my
heart's petitions.

'I will plead with God for the evangelists; I will consider the congregation at the Tabernacle, and pray that it may gently melt into the church. I will pray for the strangers who fill the aisles and crowd the pews, that God will bless them. I will say to God this day, "My God, Thou hast saved me, given me a part and lot among Thy people, and put me in Thy garden, where Thy people grow and flourish. I will not be a barren tree, but abound in fruits, especially in prayer." If I cannot do anything else I can pray. If this should be my one mite, I will put that into the treasury. I will plead with God, and give Him no rest, until He establishes His cause.'

I am not asking more of you than Jesus would ask, nor do I exact anything at your hands. Do not say, dear brother and sister, 'I hope the church will wake up.' Mind that you wake up yourself. Do not say, 'I hope they will be stirred up this morning.' Never mind others! Stir up yourself. Begin to say, 'I will join the people of God in prayer, and let them hear my voice, or at least have my presence. I will have a share in the glorious work of attracting a blessing from the skies.'

Let each one say, 'I will go also.' May God bless this word to His people, and I am sure it will result in benediction to sinners.

11

A Woman Named Damaris
Immense significance for the obscure

'Howbeit certain men clave unto him, and believed . . . and
a woman named Damaris, and others with them'
(Acts 17.34).

WE MAY READ the opening address of Paul to the philosophers on Mars' Hill *(Acts 17)*, but we cannot read
the discourse itself, for *that* was never delivered. When
Paul reached his subject, his congregation would listen no longer.
They had gratified their curiosity, and once he had made his bold
declaration concerning Jesus and the resurrection, they would hear
no more, and the meeting broke up.

Paul, no doubt, had high hopes as to the result of his reasoning
with the men of Areopagus. It was like preaching in a duke's
drawing-room to the leading spirits of society, and it was an opportunity none could despise. One would say to himself, 'What a great
occasion! God grant that much may come of it!' The results,
however, were very small. Paul gathered fewer converts out of

councillors, philosophers, and judges than he did out of the common people.

Three results followed his fragment of speech. Some mocked: these were the very learned ones, who had been pleased when he quoted one of their poets, and when he spoke of man as the offspring of God, but they had been irritated by what they considered as a ridiculous idea – the resurrection of the dead. Plato had spoken of the immortality of the soul, and on that point there was room for profound thought, but the theory of the raising of the body was beyond endurance.

When Paul spoke of a certain despised person as having risen from the dead, and asserted that this man would judge mankind, they laughed at the idea as preposterous. We hear their sarcastic words, and see their contemptuous looks, and perceive that Paul has made no impression upon them. No audience under Heaven is less likely to receive the Word than an assembly of philosophers. These receive not the wisdom of God, for they are wise in their own esteem.

A second sort did not laugh. These did not care about the matter one way or the other. As men of broad views, they were courteous, and replied to the preacher, 'We will hear thee again of this,' but most of them were probably of the same spirit as flippant Felix, who said, 'When I have a convenient season, I will call for thee.' Of this second class we have always more than of the first. They do not oppose us with mockery, but they repulse us by indifference.

Still a little handful remained to make up a third class. Paul must have greatly prized each one of that small company, and Luke, who wrote the account of the whole affair, was careful to make a full report. He mentions Dionysius the Areopagite, one of those who had made up the council before whom Paul pleaded; and he does not overlook 'a woman named Damaris'. Who she was, where she came from, and what she was like, we do not know, nor can anybody inform us; but she came forward with the few who believed, and therefore her name is written in this honourable list.

There were others; and although they were very few, a church was founded, which in due course became a power in the city, so that Paul had not laboured in vain. Thank God we are not accountable for results. If our efforts are honest and faithful, the Lord accepts them. Paul, with a heavy heart, departed from among them, but the few cheered him, and, among the rest, 'a woman named Damaris' threw in her portion of consolation. We, too, may derive benefit from her at this time.

My first observation is, that *converts are very precious in evil times.* Luke notes them particularly, as if they were jewels. Here is one, a man; yonder is another, a woman; and there are two or three others who are counted, though not named. In the day of mockery every convert was worth a Jew's eye; and this 'woman named Damaris', who might not have been remembered had she been one among the thousands of Pentecost, is specially noted among the few of Athens. Converts who dare to believe in Christ when the great mass of people reject Him are among the excellent of the earth.

Usually they are persons of a solid sort. My eyes twinkle as I read this verse – 'Howbeit certain *men* clave unto him, and believed: among the which was Dionysius the Areopagite, and a woman named Damaris.' She acted upon the inspiring exhortation, 'Quit you like men, be strong!' She is, therefore, put down among men.

Those who follow Christ when the narrow way seems altogether deserted, are people of metal. If they can go contrary to the stream they are worthy to be reckoned among true men-of-arms and choice spirits. Our converts that come to us when there is a widespread religious movement need to be watched with great care lest they should be carried off when the stream flows in the opposite direction. This 'woman named Damaris' was genuine, for she was not ashamed of the apostle when the great ones around her made him the subject of their ridicule. People who dare to confess Christ in evil times *are pretty sure to be genuine converts*. A certain class will always be mean enough to join a Christian church if they think they can get something material out of it. I have never tried to catch men with loaves and fishes, because such bait only attracts frogs, and not fish. Those who can be *bought* for church or chapel are not worth a farthing. These are not lovers of Christ's cross, but of Christ's money-bag. The 'woman named Damaris' had nothing to gain by siding with Paul. Doubtless she ran the risk of persecution. This is the style of convert we covet.

The preacher was called a fool and a babbler; but she sided with him nonetheless, and therefore she showed herself to be of that race which may be crushed, but cannot be conquered. We read of Jabez that he was more honourable than his brethren because his mother bore him with sorrow; and I believe that the converts born to the church in days of persecution are more honourable and more reliable than others.

If plants live through the winter they will not die in the spring and summer. If men and women can bear the sharp frosts of early ridicule and slander, they will easily put up with later opposition, and will endure even to the end. It is very important that all additions to our church should be of the right kind. I try to exercise, together with my elders, as great caution as is consistent with charity; but do what we may we are deceived by those who say that they are Christ's, and are not. I feel, however, pretty sure of those who come to us in the teeth of opposition.

Such persons as this 'woman named Damaris' are specially valuable, because they are generally *people of vigorous spiritual life*. Paul had only two or three converts at Athens, but he might well have taken comfort from the old Greek fable of the fox and the lioness. The fox boasted of the number of her cubs, and taunted the lioness because she had but one. 'Yes,' said the lioness, 'but that one is a lion.' I venture to believe that the very fact that Damaris is here recorded implies that she was well known in those days. It was impossible to omit her name as she had written it too clearly upon the hearts of the saints. I am certain that those who come to Christ when few are coming, and confess the faith in the midst of opposition, are the people who will leave deep footprints, whose influence will abide.

This little note which constitutes my text also shows me that *converts are all valued by the Holy Spirit,* and by the church of God. Observe that we have here the honourable name of 'Dionysius the Areopagite'. There are many legends about him, none of which I believe, and therefore I shall not repeat them, but he was evidently a man of consequence, for he was one of the notable council of Areopagus. But, strangely, next to him is 'a woman named Damaris' of whom the best biblical dictionaries say, 'Nothing whatever is known of this person.' Her name, however, is not left out, but recorded alongside noble Dionysius. Grace creates true 'liberty, equality, and fraternity'.

Saints are individually chosen, beloved, redeemed; called by the Spirit of God, put into the family of love, made joint-heirs with Jesus, and they shall all reign with Him for ever and ever. All are equally written in the Lamb's book of life.

Observe that *sex is no detriment.* How greatly God has blessed women in the midst of His Church! They have been highly favoured in their happy and holy experiences. If they were first in the transgression, they were last at the cross, and first at the sepulchre; and no woman ever betrayed her Lord, or even denied Him, these latter disgraces being left for men. I know of no wrong of such a kind that is recorded of the female discipleship in the New Testament.

There are sinners mentioned whom Christ made His disciples, but these loved much, and were the companions of those who ministered to Him of their substance. Woman is raised to her right place by the tender hand of Him Who was 'born of a woman'.

Obscurity also does not diminish the value of a believer. What if we know nothing about 'a woman named Damaris'? The Lord will still have her name emblazoned in the roll of His chosen. My dear friend! You may have very little talent, scant wealth, and no fame – hidden away among the masses – but if you are a believer, you are on the roll of the armies of the Lord, and in that great day your name shall not be missed at the final muster.

No sort of singularity shall make the believer of any less value. I do not know that there is much in it, but the woman's name, according to Cruden, means 'little woman'. Read for Damaris, 'little lady'. I have known, in the church of God, little men like Zacchaeus, and little women like Damaris, and yet they have been great in the kingdom of Heaven.

I have known persons physically impaired, who were spiritually beautiful. They were the very life of the meetings for prayer – diligent as Dorcas, loving as Lydia, holy as Hannah, mothers in Israel like Deborah. Many a minister has said, 'I do not know what we should do without that little woman.' So, too, many a brother who has been lame or blind has, despite his infirmity, been a man of great mind, and God has greatly blessed him. Dr Isaac Watts, the poet of the sanctuary, was a little man; and when he was spoken of in slighting terms, he said –

> *Were I so tall to reach the pole,*
> *Or grasp the ocean with my span,*
> *I must be measured by my soul,*
> *The mind's the standard of the man.*

When you give your heart to Jesus, do not imagine for a moment that He will despise you because you are not a great lady, or a person of consequence. Do not fret because the pastor scarcely knows you among so many. How can he know everybody? He would willingly be the shepherd of you all; but if he cannot be, remember that the

Lord Jesus Christ, that great Shepherd of the sheep, will gladly fold you among His blood-bought flock.

Your lot is obscure, your name is unspoken; you are little in presence, little in business, little in ability, little in every way; but the Lord despises not one of those little ones which believe in Him. Thus has 'a woman named Damaris' taught us two truths. The most precious converts are those brought in in dark times, but none of them may at any time be lightly esteemed.

Another truth in this text is that *converts exhibit much the same marks.* No two converts are quite alike, and yet certain distinguishing marks are always seen in them. Note that it is written, 'Howbeit certain men *clave unto him.*' They clave unto the despised preacher of Christ. Conversion frequently begins in this way. There is a cleaving, first of all, to the preacher himself, because he speaks the Truth, and then a cleaving to the Truth which he speaks. What he has said has come home to the hearer's heart, and so he resolves to hear more of it, and to keep coming to the services. This cleaving to the preacher, if it be of the right sort, is really a cleaving to the preacher's Lord. I am glad when people become camp followers, for I feel they may soon enlist as soldiers of the cross.

Better still, we find that *they believed.* It would have been of no use cleaving to Paul if they had not believed the Gospel: but this they did. They trusted in the Son of God, Who rose from the dead. They left their idols and their good works, and placed their hope in the ascended Saviour. They believed. This was the great turning-point.

What did they do next? *They came forward and confessed their faith.* Does a reader say – 'That is not in the text'? How could Luke have written down the name of 'a woman named Damaris' if she had not avowed her faith? She joined the flock, and became a partaker of the sufferings of the followers of Jesus. She owned herself a Christian, and took the consequences. This is the mark of true converts. They cannot hide their love, but openly confess it. The verse before us reads like an extract from the church book of Athens. If you meet a Christian who has never joined a church you may call him a stray Christian.

Last of all, our text reminds us that *true converts are made useful.* 'That also is not in the text,' someone protests. It may not be in the words of the text, but this sermon is a proof of it. 'A woman named Damaris', of whom we know so little, brings glory to God at this very hour by what little we do know of her. She clave to Paul, she believed, and she confessed Christ in that dark day; and now, at this hour, she 'being dead yet speaketh'. She speaks to us all the more because of her obscurity.

This woman has spoken to me many a time for years. Often when I have been reading the Scriptures to myself a whisper has said, 'Preach a sermon upon "a woman named Damaris".' I have said to myself, 'I do not know anything about her.' At last it came to my mind that this was the beauty of the case. Say that Jesus Christ saves people of whom nobody knows anything. Talk of her of whom nothing is known except that she clave to Paul and believed in Jesus Christ. Many who will hear or read the sermon will be like her, and God will bless the word to their comfort.

Damaris speaks to the encouragement of humble persons, lowly, and unknown. *You may come to Christ.* I dread lest any of you should think that you must be of importance before you can be saved. We are all important to Christ because we have immortal souls. If you swept a crossing and were clothed with rags you might believe and live. It is the soul that the Lord cares for, not the trappings. Come to Jesus, whoever you may be. Seek His face and trust Him, because this humble woman named Damaris did so. In this way she is useful many long years after her death.

You that are saved, but remain unknown, *do not wish to be known.* How often have I longed that I could get where I should not be treated as a public exhibition! You live under a glass case when once you are a public character. Everybody pries even into your domestic life; and falsehoods buzz about you like wasps. Do not court publicity, nor crave popularity. Be quite satisfied to do your duty and serve your God, and never to be heard of; for the less you are heard of, and the less you are known, the more peaceful will your life be. If nobody praises you, why do you want to be praised? 'A woman named Damaris' lost nothing by being unknown. Holy actions are spoiled if we wish them to be seen.

I know a friend who wanted to give a present to another on her birthday, and the chosen article was bought secretly, but somehow it came to be seen by the person for whom it was intended, and the pleasure was spoiled. When you do anything for Jesus, do it by stealth. Hide your left hand behind you, and do not let it know what your right hand is doing.

There is a certain bloom upon the fruit of grace which is the beauty of it. A single intrusive hand may rub it off. Like 'a woman named Damaris' keep yourself unknown if you can serve Jesus the better for it. You shall be remembered, and your name shall be recorded, and you shall have your reward from the Lord alone. If you seek the applause of men, you have your reward, and a poor recompense it is, but if you serve the Lord Christ, and wish only to be known of Him Who seeth in secret, then your reward shall be great.

I have done. What I have been aiming at all the while is that I may cheer you into the courage which will make you confess your Lord. You will increase the number of the church by one, and that is something great, if done for Christ's sake. We seek not yours, but you. We want 'a woman named Damaris', though she has no long purse, nor long tongue, and no long train. Jesus Christ wants her, though she is not wealthy, nor beautiful, nor forward. Oh, that she might be led to say, 'That blessed Saviour shall have my trust, and I will be His servant evermore. Write my name down along with "a woman named Damaris"!' Come, and welcome, you hidden ones, for Jesus saith: 'Him that cometh to me I will in no wise cast out.'

(A short address in *The Sword & the
Trowel,* May 1889, not included in the
Metropolitan Tabernacle Pulpit.)